SCHOLARS TEAMING TO ALLEVIATE RACISM IN SOCIETY (STARS)

SCHOLARS TEAMING TO ALLEVIATE RACISM IN SOCIETY (STARS)

Edited by
Rose Marie Duhon-Sells
Alice Marie Duhon-Ross
and
Gwendolyn Mary Duhon

The Edwin Mellen Press

Library of Congress Cataloging-in-Publication Data

Scholars teaming to alleviate racism in society (STARS) / edited by Rose Marie Duhon-Sells, Alice Marie Duhon-Ross, Gwendolyn Mary Duhon.
    p. cm.
  Includes bibliographical references.
  ISBN 0-7734-7510-9
  1. Racism. 2. Race relations. 3. Racism--United States. 4. United States--Race relations. I. Duhon-Sells, Rose M. II. Duhon-Ross, Alice. III. Duhon, Gwendolyn M.

HT1521 .S325 2001
305.8'00973--dc21   00-048719

A CIP catalog record for this book is available from the British Library.

The Edwin Mellen Press   The Edwin Mellen Press
Box 450   Box 67
Lewiston, New York   Queenston, Ontario
USA 14092-0450   CANADA L0S 1L0

The Edwin Mellen Press, Ltd.
Lampeter, Ceredigion, Wales
UNITED KINGDOM SA48 8LT

TABLE OF CONTENTS

PREFACE
A BRIEF DESCRIPTION OF
SCHOLARS TEAMING TO ALLEVIATE
RACISM IN SOCIETY
(STARS)

William Kritsonis, PhD
McNeese State University
Lake Charles, Louisiana

This book deals with effective approaches and ideas for dealing with issues related to racism in the community, homes, schools, agencies, and society. The 15 chapters are written by authors who represent diversified cultural backgrounds and life experiences.

The book will serve as an excellent supplemental teaching guide for educators, teachers, principals, superintendents, supervisors, consultants, community leaders, school board members, government officials, and parents. College professors will find the diverse content of this book both thought-provoking and stimulating for their students. The information will strengthen the fiber of courses and deeply broaden multicultural diversified perspectives.

It is interesting to note that this book is written by a wide cross-section of individuals. Seventy-five percent of the chapters were written by Caucasians, while 25% are authored by people of color. Readers should remember the content of the book is from a broad range of individuals representing widely diversified cultural perspectives.

The first chapter was written by Susan H. Horwitz. Susan describes racism as she experienced it while growing up in a sheltered and privileged family. She provides strategies and techniques for people to utilize in becoming enlightened human beings who are capable of learning from every individual they meet.

The second chapter was written by Rochelle Carr Burns. Rochelle presents a chronological history of racism from the perspective of a Canadian. She provides a penetrating rationale for a change from racism to cooperation and learning from each other.

The third chapter was written by Mary Ann Jansen. This interesting chapter focuses on the racial issues involved with the Catholic Church and the life experiences of a nun. Mary Ann recommends that people deal with racism in a positive manner and explains why students must learn to appreciate each other.

The fourth chapter was written by Ronald Goldman. This chapter looks at racism from the perspective of a leader in business and industry. In addition, attitudes toward infants, mother-child relationships, self-esteem, disruptive bonding, and traumatic issues are presented.

The fifth chapter was written by Janet Avery. This chapter focuses on a woman who was a changed agent in dealing with racism. Janet has had a tremendous impact on healing racism throughout New York City.

The sixth chapter was written by Jeff Garrett and Glenn Doston. This chapter was developed by a team that included a university professor and a minister, one African American, and one Caucasian. Ideas are presented for helping students to better understand attitudes towards racism.

The seventh chapter was written by W. Henry Alderfer and Lauren Alderfer. The chapter focuses on how individuals of two different countries deal with race interaction and racial tension. The countries are Ecuador and El Salvador.

The eighth chapter was written by Amelia Gross. It deals with an individual who used the strategies and techniques of Ella Roosevelt to address racism in both the military and civilian life. The author's main goals are to stamp out racism as a white person and focus on the human gifts.

The ninth chapter was written by Bethe Hagens. This chapter describes aspects of socialization beginning in the 60s through to the present focusing on positive methods of how racism may be alleviated through communication. The author also focuses on eliminating racism from a personal perspective.

The 10th chapter was written by Cynthia L. Jackson. This chapter deals with the rise of the black American from slavery to citizenship. The power of racism, acceptance, alleviating racism, and many other issues are discussed.

The 11th chapter was written by Angela C. May. The information in this chapter is from the perspective of a person growing up in Detroit, Michigan. Angela emphasizes how strong family units help children to develop without being paralyzed by racism.

The 12th chapter was written by Frances V. Rains. This author is a Native American professor at Penn State University. Frances presents interrelated issues that impact the future.

The 13th chapter was written by Maria Love. This chapter is a beautiful story written by a Caucasian woman who learned about racism from personal experiences. Individuals were not aware of the pain she experienced as a result of misinformation.

The 14th chapter was written by Celina Echols. This chapter focuses on the life struggles of a young woman who grew up in Mississippi. She learned early that quitting is not an option for those who want to be successful in life.

The 15th and final chapter was written by Neil Faulk. This chapter provides a penetrating perspective regarding standardized testing. The author recommends ways to make standardized test results more inclusive, rather than exclusive in the evaluation of students from diversified cultural backgrounds.

In conclusion, this book represents the views of a wide range of writers from diverse cultural backgrounds and life experiences. The book is an excellent resource for those serious individuals who want to make a difference in helping to solve many lingering problems associated with racism in our global society.

FOREWORD

Edward L. Wingard
Dean/Professor, Emeritus
The Union Institute
Cincinnati, Ohio

One of the great tragedies of civilization has been its continuing inability to grapple with race and ethnicity. Racism appears to be institutionalized in the United States, as well as in many parts of the world. Rage over racism is inexplicably tied to the social and political fabric of society. This racism is the product of the anger, violence, hatred, and indifference between and amongst groups and individuals. The distinguished and eminent scholar, William E. B. DuBois, was correct in asserting "that the problem of the twentieth century is the problem of the color line–the relation of the darker to the lighter races of men in Asia and Africa, in America and the islands of the sea." The population of the world today is almost four times as large as when these words were written in 1903, and many would say that the problem of racism is also four times as large!

Around the world, the conversations and debates on the subjects of race, justice, equality, and freedom have occupied the attention of thousands of honorable men and women. It is significant to note that most of these "drum majors for justice" represent the church and/or the school, and consider their mission as ordained duty. The teaching profession in the United States is known for its efforts to promote values and ethics through student learning. Thus, it is not surprising that substantial changes in our society began in schools and on college campuses. Names such as Little Rock, Orangeburg Selma, Montgomery, Boston, Antioch, Oberlin, Kent State, and Jackson State, all conjure images of student protests and demonstrations for civil and human rights, and much of the passion for these struggles was developed by educators and parishioners.

This collection of manuscripts by college professors and doctoral students was developed to address racism throughout society. The authors are different in that they represent diversity in all respects, yet they are alike in that they abhor all manifestations of racism. This collaborative project seeks to alleviate the effects of racism by offering a scholarly contribution for others, particularly those associated with the development and care of children. The chapters in the book reflect the thinking and practices of authors from a cross-section of the world. Their intent is to underscore the obvious–racism is epidemic, and we must address this problem now; we must save the children; we must assess our belief and value systems; and we must work to save ourselves before it is too late.

DuBois spoke about the 20th century. These authors have chosen to speak proactively about the 21st century, with the goal of eradicating racism through scholarship. In a real sense, far too little progress has been made in race relations. It is high time for all of us to manage this major social problem with real authority and sanity. We must work to abolish racism in all of its insidious forms. The messages presented here are descriptive of the belief systems, attitudes, and values that are required to accomplish this task. This important conversation must continue until it becomes a parade of joyful confidence in the mission of eradicating racism. Our common future will be determined by our collective responses in this matter.

INTRODUCTION

Rose M. Duhon-Sells, Editor
The Union Institute, Cincinnati, Ohio

Alice Duhon-Ross, Editor
Albany State University, Albany, Georgia

Gwendolyn Duhon, Editor
McNeese State University, Lake Charles, Louisiana

S cholars Teaming to Alleviate Racism (STARS) is a manuscript that resulted from a discussion at The Union Institutes' graduate school colloquium for doctorate students. The colloquium was a multiracial, multicultural and multi-faceted group of individuals from various academic and economic backgrounds. The people in the group all shared a common concern about the detrimental impact of racism on the growth and progress of this society. Whites and people of color were asking the same question, "What can we do to stop the growing epidemic of racism in this society?" The vast majority of people in this nation want to see the end of racism, but few are courageous enough to take the risk of speaking out against it. The fear of many people is that they will be ostracized by those who are the racist gatekeepers–who may treat them the way people of color are treated. They know racism is wrong and there is pain in their hearts when they witness racist behavior and remain silent

The contributors to this book are of the highest quality of professional human beings in this nation. Their major purpose for writing chapters for this document is to improve the quality of life for all by focusing on changing themselves in an effort to facilitate change in others.

The group decided to contribute their personal stories, reflecting their personal experiences. They were asked to respond to the following topics:

- At what age did you become aware of racial differences among people?
- What was your first experience with racism and its impact on your perception about skin color?
- As an adult what are your perceptions of racism and how have they changed?
- How are you contributing to the alleviation of racism in your environment?

The new century is upon us and America is still fighting the age-old battle of racism. In 1902, the black scholar W.E.B. DuBois forecasted that "The problem of the 20th century is the problem of the color line. The question is how far differences of a race, which show themselves chiefly in the color of the skin and the texture of the hair, will hereafter be made the basis of denying over half the world the right of sharing to their ability the opportunity and privileges of modern civilization." To this day the terminology has changed to current terms such as "Redling," "Steering," or "racial profiling." The stakes are higher now and the suffering is greater.

Unfortunately, the power and control are still held in the hands of racist individuals who rationalize their actions by living in denial about their contribution to the suffering and pain of this nation, caused by the haters. The real pain and suffering is imposed on our children because they are often taught by the fear and hate adults in their immediate environments are practicing.

Mother Teresa said the greatest disease from which the human race is suffering is not cancer or AIDS, but the feeling of being unwanted or unloved. Loving your "brother" is at the core of every major faith in the world today. Yet, the simplicity of that edict has eluded humanity since the beginning of time. Until we can simply reach out our hands and acknowledge one another without regard to race, separation seems our destiny. How does this apply to you?

1. A simple "hello" is the most basic thing you can do--not just to those you are accustomed to greeting, but individuals outside of your own race, creed, or color as well. A simple verbal "hello," a wave of the hand, or more importantly, to look into the eyes of an individual, allowing that person the dignity of being acknowledged, is more important than starting a foundation or donating money to any cause pertaining to racism.
2. Acknowledge and develop an appreciation for the legacy and achievements of another race, creed, or color. We have to be willing to give dignity and credence to the lives of others. Most people define themselves by their origins, so acknowledging another culture's importance and place in history is the beginning of your acceptance of someone outside of your own race, creed, or color as different, but equal.

The contents of this book will help everyone who reads it to realize that the alleviation of racism is the responsibility of all human beings. The key is to start with yourself and reach one person at a time.

CHAPTER 1
A JOURNEY TOWARD
ENLIGHTENMENT

Susan H. Horwitz
University of Rochester Medical Center
Rochester, New York

I was born and raised in Syracuse, New York. My parents were quiet people with solid values and strict rules that translated into expectations for my sister and me; expectations to be good citizens, work hard, get a good education, marry, and instill their values in their progeny, our children. My parents didn't discuss politics or economics very often. They certainly didn't discuss race, class, or culture, at least not in an intellectual or academic manner.

Every once in a while, when a house was being sold in our neighborhood, my father would say, "We don't want blacks in this neighborhood. The property values will drop!" On the issue of being Jewish, he would say, "Be proud to be a Jew. Know who you are, but don't flaunt it–no jewelry with Jewish stars or mezuzahs!" When I look back, I think my father was afraid of racial and religious differences–ours and "theirs." I am sure he had no idea how painful the African American experience was, or how to incorporate a multicultural world into his vision of family and neighborhood.

Then there was the issue of context. I was born in 1947. Those were difficult times for Jews. There was anti-Semitic sentiment, though not very overt in my memory. Jews were recovering from the shock of the Holocaust and terrified that such violence against our people could and might happen any time; sooner than later. Maintaining safety, be it physical, psychological, or emotional was held as an important value. Jewish professionals, lawyers, like my Dad, had to work hard to earn people's respect and trust. My father carried himself with dignity and guided us with what appeared to be assurance, but he was, more than likely, fraught with anxiety.

We lived within the city limits, on the urban "fringe." I don't remember seeing any black or Hispanic children in my elementary school. I grew up safe, protected from trauma, and privileged as a white child in a loving family never exposed in depth to other cultures. I knew different religions, religious beliefs, and how churches and synagogues were dissimilar. But, I knew nothing about racial differences, other than the obvious different colors of skin.

My parents liked to travel. They took my sister and me with them on many trips. There was irony in that they viewed travel as an educational experience, yet underexposed us to racial and class tensions within the cultures we visited. We traveled to Florida many times to visit my mother's parents. We spent six weeks exploring California, Oregon, Washington, and the Canadian Rockies when I was 11 years old. My parents took me to Europe at age 16. There were many trips to various states within the US. Through all that exposure, there was never a discussion about race, or the effects of racial differences on all of us. To say that I was raised in a cocoon, free from violence, free from trauma, free from curiosity and concern about other races and classes is an immutable fact. Maintaining safety and going about our business was the message about how life was to be lived.

In the decades that passed since my childhood and adolescence, I have learned about racial differences. My values (and my parents' values) related to honesty, the work ethic, generosity of spirit (and money—what we call tzedakah), and being a good citizen have all withstood the challenges of person, place, and time. In some ways, I picked up the banner my parents passed to me and continued by bringing our family to a more informed place. I traveled with my husband and our children. To our Sabbath table, I brought ethical dilemmas raised by social issues of the day. I challenged my own preconceived notions about the separate world of blacks and whites, entertaining similarities; actually searching for similarities. I did not want to feel my father's fear about racial or religious differences. I wanted to feel comfortable with blacks, with other races and religions and, mostly, with myself. I thought I was "on target" until I began my doctoral studies at The Union Institute. Now I know I have not even scratched the surface.

Exposure Brings Pain

A videotape entitled *The Color of Fear* jolted me from my comfortable, intellectual understanding of racism. The group of men from different racial backgrounds portrayed in this film spent a weekend together in a cabin discussing race, its meaning, and implications for the quality of life. They confronted one another, dispelled myths, dismantled stereotypes, dislodged time-held beliefs, sometimes yelling, sometimes crying, and finally breaking through the glass-wall barriers between and among them. I found myself disturbed by their struggles and realized that I, too, was struggling with some of the same presuppositions.

Recently accepted to the doctoral program at The Union Institute, I attended a colloquium, which orientated new learners. The videotape was shown at this meeting to broaden our perspective as future academics. The discussion that followed was lively and intense. Nine of the 13 new learners decided to continue the discussion via electronic communication after we returned home. Part of the program's residency requirement is to participate in 10 "peer days" throughout the doctoral program, which can be accomplished in person with learners in close proximity to the learner's home, or through The Union Institute's website services. For two weeks we e-mailed one another, planning the structure of our peer day. We found it difficult to focus on procedures, preferring to write to each other about racism. We spent 10 days on-line, instead of the required eight days. Feeling insatiable, we concluded we would organize a second peer day one month later. Five of the original nine learners reconvened for that second dialogue.

Those two peer days were critically important for me. We shared personal stories of our experiences with racism. We exchanged thoughts and ideas about the books and articles we had chosen to read. Stories that exposed pain and fear of persecution and rejection crossed our computer screens. Admissions of rage and helplessness, as well as faux pas and racial errors of our own were shared and described. As a social action project that reflected each of our ideas, we formulated a seminar on racism viewed from a multidisciplinary perspective (music, medicine, corporate America, and mental health) to offer fellow learners with the guidance of our mentor, Rose Duhon-Sells, PhD.

Many nights I lay awake thinking about the electronic exchanges I had had with my cybernetically connected colleagues. The more we worked, the more deeply saddened I became. This racism "thing" was no longer an intellectual exercise. It was real and frightening. I *did not* feel comfortable any longer. I *did* feel my father's fear of differences, though for different reasons.

My new knowledge, laced with sadness and concern for people of color, their experiences, and all of our futures, was informing me about the work I was doing with non-custodial fathers in a project that assessed father programs, and in my work with partner violence. The former involvement had to do with a grant from local funders that put me in touch with fathers of all races and socioeconomic strata, as well as program directors, staff, and clients of these programs. I administered surveys, conducted interviews, and participated in groups as a guest speaker. The latter work with partner violence was the brainchild I invented to create a context for my doctoral research–a specialty clinic within our primary mental clinic where trainees and I assess and treat aggressive and abusive couples of all races, ethnicities, and socioeconomic strata.

The peer day and my clinical and community work taught me a lot about institutionalized racism, a societal belief that denies people of color access to the economic, educational, and social pathways to growth and change. I began to understand how our larger societal structures were shaping the attitudes and belief systems that kept black and Hispanic men and women from achieving a sense of dignity, respect, and self-esteem (Brice-Baker, 1994; Oliver, 1999; West, 1994). For example, Brice-Baker, in her article entitled "Domestic Violence in African American and African-Caribbean Families" stated, "The aggressive stereotype, animalistic and primitive, is viewed as part of the culture and the black man's nature. Blacks viewed as poor and crime-centered with disorganized family structures lead to low self-esteem, as individuals, families, and as a society." Brice-Baker presents the notion that black and Hispanic men incorporated these beliefs into their own ideas about themselves. There were economic realities that reinforced the stereotypes, driving many unskilled and undereducated men of color underground to create economies of scale that would support their families, while giving them a feeling of success. This interpretation of one outcome of institutionalized racism rang true during a therapy session I recently held in my family therapy practice. The mixed-race male partner (African American, Hispanic, and Native American) was telling his Caucasian girlfriend and mother of two of his five children that he could not meet his financial obligations to all his children, to her, and to their home. He anguished as he told her in session that she demanded too much from him (time and money). He reported how his friend was dealing drugs and that's how "his woman" got her new clothes and clothes for the children. My client worked nights, sometimes two shifts, and still could not make enough money to break even. He was thinking that he may begin "dealing," too. "At least I'd get you off my back," he told her.

Clarity Emerges Through Education

Men in Rochester's father programs (both urban and suburban) lament about the gender biases they face in the courts as they fight for their rights to parent their children. Approximately 85% to 90% of all custody cases are resolved out of court with primary residence awarded to mothers. Though joint custody and shared residence is increasing, mothers continue to be seen as primary caretakers. Interestingly, the 10% to 15% of cases that go to trial result in fathers gaining primary custody/residence in 90% of those cases.

More recent data from a developing national study of unmarried fathers (McLanahan, 1998) reveal that, of unmarried fathers under 30 years of age are as follows:

- 82% of these fathers are romantically involved with the mothers of their children.
- 52% cohabitate with the mother.
- 50% intend to marry the mother (as reported to the researcher at the time of the birth of their first child).
- 85% plan to declare paternity and put their names on the birth certificate.
- 78% helped during pregnancy.

In this same study only 6% of the mothers did not want the fathers involved in their lives. This study, funded by the Ford Foundation, is a 20-city project. The results listed above reflect data from two (of 20) cities studied thus far (McLanahan, 1998). "The fathers in this study are clearly motivated to be responsible and present when their children are born" (McLanahan, 1998).

Why should a father who so desperately wants to be a significant and meaningful person in his children's lives be denied access to those children who need him (Popenoe, 1996)? The marginalization of black and Hispanic men is a crime. Further the marginalization of black and Hispanic fathers is a violent act inflicted upon their young children and men of all races because these acts of disempowerment deprive their future generations of dignity and quality of life. This systematic disconnection between men of color and their families is sinful, dangerous, and must not be tolerated.

Charles Derber's book, **The Wilding of America: How Greed and Violence Are Eroding Our Nation's Character**, is a poignant and articulate discussion of my stay-awake thoughts and fears. Derber took me into my fears while simultaneously predicting the future, my grandchildren's future. While he promotes the notion of individualism as a valued sociopolitical stance that advances individual growth and prosperity, he draws the distinction between individualism and wilding. Wilding refers to a state of individualism that results in violent acts (emotionally, financially, and psychologically violent, as well as physically violent) against others. In other words, self gain at the expense of another. He moved me well beyond my personal thoughts into a metaperspective on racism. He created a sociopolitical and economic picture that brought clarity to the underpinnings of institutionalized racism; the contorted and "dysfunctional definitions of manhood facing men and sons of color" (Oliver, 1999).

"Crime is a product of a disparity between goals and means. If that disparity becomes institutionalized, crime and other deviance is normalized, and officially deviant behavior becomes common practice. Wilding itself becomes a societal way of life" (Derber, 1996). Fathers have rights, but the possibilities of overcoming the obstacles and removing the barriers in order to achieve those rights are often insurmountable for too many fathers due to lack of funds to "fight the fight" or high levels of frustration turned into despair. The crime against fathers, the deprivation of paternal rights, particularly of black fathers, is a reflection of Derber's construct of institutional wilding. Since wilding is permitted in all our institutions, we are all affected. We are all in danger and we should all be afraid.

The exquisitely formulated perspectives on the Rodney King beating, trial, and post-trial riots articulately described by a collection of authors in Gooding-Williams's book, **Reading Rodney King: Reading Urban Uprising**, so aptly uncovered ambivalence (in some cases) and sheer racism (in other cases) of the white community (Gooding-Williams, 1993). Perhaps we whites are afraid to look at ourselves for fear we might see our black brothers and sisters in ourselves. What are we whites so afraid to see? Pain? Vulnerability? Fear itself? Black people's pain must be felt as our pain. Their rage must be experienced as our rage. "Expressive and instru-mental wilding have in common an antisocial self-centeredness made possible by a stunning collapse of moral restraints and a chilling lack of empathy" (Derber, 1996). Who are we kidding? We are all in this together. If we "go down" in anarchy, de-struction, and retribution, we "go down" together. *Or*, as Derber writes in his last chapter:

> As we consider rewriting the dream for a better future, we have consolation that we can look to our history for guidance. Through most of America's past, the purely materialistic and individualistic side of the dream has been balanced by a moral and community oriented side, preventing the dream from transmut-ing into a wilding recipe. Moreover, the dream has been inclusive, defining a set of common purposes to which all Americans could aspire. These historical features of the dream need to be recaptured in order to fortify civil society and purge the wilding epidemic (Derber, 1996).

Ruth Wilson Gilmore (1993), Derber (1996), and others write about the hope and possibilities for the future: a civil society, new types of politicians with visions for all people, a new ethic of relatedness, and empathy across all races, classes, and cultures. Do we have the courage to stand up and say, "This racism and promulga-tion of poverty, want, and abandon is wrong?" The opportunity for change knocks at our door. I, for one, intend to ask, "Who's there?" and then, let the new day enter.

References

Brice-Baker, J.R. (1994). *Domestic violence in African American and African-Caribbean families*. **Journal of Social Distress and the Homeless**, *3*(1), 23-37.

Derber, C. (1996). **The wilding of America: How greed and violence are eroding our nation's character**. New York: St. Martin's Press.

Gilmore, R.W. (1993). *Terror austerity race gender excess theater*. In R. Gooding-Williams (Ed.), **Reading Rodney King: Reading urban uprising**. New York: Routledge, Inc.

Gooding-Williams, R. (Ed.). (1993). **Reading Rodney King: Reading urban uprising**. New York: Routledge, Inc.

McLanahan, S. (1998). **A 20-city study funded by The Ford Foundation with two cities completed**. Report given at the "Summit of Urban Fathers," sponsored by the National Fatherhood Initiative, June 14, 1999, Washington, DC.

Popenoe, D. (1996). **Life without father**. New York: The Free Press.

Oliver, W. (1999). **Violent black men: The rationale for culturally competent interven-tions**. A presentation given at the 6th International Family Violence Research Confer-ence, July 27, 1999, University of New Hampshire, Durham, New Hampshire.

West, C. (1994). **Race matters**. New York: Vantage Press.

CHAPTER 2
HISTORY AND RACISM:
WHAT ALWAYS WAS, IS.
BUT NEED IT BE?

Rochelle Carr Burns
The Union Institute
Cincinnati, Ohio

O ne thing history has proven about racism is that it has always existed in some form. Names identifying discriminatory acts have changed. The in-groups and outgroups have been altered periodically. But, the one thing that remains constant is that prejudiced[1] conduct and its consequent deleterious effects remain historically omnipresent.

Throughout North American history, the cry has continuously been heard, "This is the worst of times for racism." Again, at the end of this century, we read the words: "Many Americans seem to be moving toward increasing indifference to others. Intolerance–even outright hatred–of people who are 'different' is on the rise" (Cohen, 1998, p. ix). The problem with this clarion call is that it could have been written in South Carolina in 1860, in New York City in 1920, in the Province of Québec in 1980, or at any other time in this continent's history. The topic of racism, with its lack of a base in logic, is difficult enough to fathom. Added to this conundrum is the belief that we are living in a time that is different from any other time. That is not so.

What fuels the fire of confusion surrounding racism are three points: the changing historical terminology, the lack of a universally accepted definition of who belongs to what "race," and the absence of a consensus as to how many "races" exist.

---

[1] The term, "prejudice," is used in this chapter in its negative connotation.

According to Bryant, at present there could be up to nine races. There is the European "white" Caucasian, from Scandinavia to the Mediterranean, Southern Europe and Northern Africa; the African, from south of the Sahara; the Asian, from continental Asia, but excluding South Asia and the Middle East, but including people of China, Japan, Taiwan, Indonesia, the Philippines, and from the India-Pakistan subcontinent, although the latter is sometimes treated as a separate group; the American Indian, also known as Amerindian and American Mongoloid; and the Pacific group, consisting of four groups that are taken together or sometimes separate, which include the Australian aborigine; the Melanesian, the Polynesian, and the Micronesian.

Despite the confusing designations, North Americans certainly understand the word "racism" in terms of its power to divide humans into various ingroups and outgroups. They also understand other divisive terms that are used separately from or synonymously with "racism." Such terms as xenophobia, gay-bashing, anti-Semitism, anti-feminism, and every other possible "anti-" linked with every other possible outgroup are both a part of historical writing and present day news events. In essence, the problem is that throughout North American history the term, or a comparable one, has been used pejoratively in a political and cultural context, with massive injurious social consequences.

For example, in the 18th and 19th centuries, the African continent and its inhabitants were seized for economic reasons. The former fact would become monumentally important to the United States. Justification for grabbing the people and property was based, at first, not on the term "race," but on the fact they were "heathens." With the waning of religious power by the late 18th century, the pretext for such action was found in the term "race." In his seminal work, *The Nature of Prejudice,* Gordon Allport pointed out:

> The simplicity of "race" gave an immediate and visible mark, so it was thought, by which to designate victims of dislike. And the fixation of racial inferiority became, so it seemed, an irrefutable justification for prejudice. It had the stamp of biological finality, and spared people the pain of examining the complex economic, cultural, political, and psychological conditions that enter into group relations (Bryant, 1994, p. 3).

At various times in my life, the myopia of the bigot has affected me, both as a Jew and as a woman. The story of the Jews is probably the preeminent example in the annals of history of an on-going targeted group. In his best-selling book, Cahill (1998) noted:

> Our history is replete with examples of those who have refused to see what the Jews are really about, who–through intellectual blindness, racial chauvinism, xenophobia, or just plain evil–have been unable to give this odd ball tribe, this raggle-taggle band, this race of wanderers who are the progenitors of the Western world, their due. Indeed, at the end of this bloodiest of centuries, we can all

too easily look back on scenes of unthinkable horror perpetuated by those who would do anything rather than give the Jews their due. (pp. 3-4)

The reasons, once again, tell more about those holding the prejudice and about the historical milieu in which they lived than about being Jewish and it was the same for me. At Graduate School at the University of Toronto in the early 1970s, two other students and I were talking about the "non-helpfulness" of one professor. "What do you expect," said the other two, 'he's a Jew." Whatever it meant to "look" like a Jew, I did not qualify in their eyes. I was not only totally accepted by them, but they constantly sought me out. My presence was completely wanted because of my personality, the same personality that would have been overlooked had the religion of my birth been known.

I argued that we all didn't like this man because of the personality he chose to exhibit. The fact that he was a Jew, I contended, was irrelevant, especially in light of the fact that the other professors who were Jewish we all liked. What hit me with the force of a thunderbolt was not the prejudice. I had been mistaken for being non-Jewish before. The shock was that this man and woman, both well educated, were visible minorities. One would think that having gone through the pain, victims of an outgroup would have the answers, or at least the sensitivity to try to end this debilitating system. This was not so. Far too often throughout North American history, the oppressed have oppressed others or factions within their own group they deemed weaker.

What is also sadly noteworthy, just as those two graduate students displayed, is that there are examples throughout history of convenient partial prejudice. As Weeks (1995) pointed out:

Rights do not exist in nature. They are products of social relations and of changing historical circumstances and balance of forces, so the claim for rights is always in terms of some rights rather than others. (p. 119)

Often throughout history, dealings with an outgroup constituted discrimination and acceptance at the same time. During World War II, when democracies, including the United States, were fighting for their very way of being, the American armed forces accepted both blacks and whites, but not without overt discrimination. Although the populace was united in fear, it was not until after the War that the armed forces were desegregated by President Harry S. Truman. This situation shows two things. First, the best of intentions is not enough. Laws are necessary to give power to those with the best of intentions in order to keep those without the best of intentions in line. Second, the one thing inherent in prejudice, as seen throughout history, is its lack of logic.

Personal stories and historical examples are forever entwined, as well they should be. History is, after all, the recollection of many personal and group stories. The following two illustrations bear this out. On February 28, 1877, the House of Representatives received the "Report of the Joint Special Committee to Investigate

Chinese Immigration." It read, in part: "The deduction from the testimony taken by the committee . . . would seem to be that there is not sufficient brain capacity in the Chinese to furnish motive power for self-government" (Jacobson, 1998, pp. 158-159). One hundred years later, I was offered a job to mediate social differences between groups moving into a Toronto suburban development. In spite of the fact that three of the most prominent figures within Canada's largest development company asked me to take the job, the offer was rescinded the following week. I learned that these three men met with those with whom I would be working in the company. The all male group vetoed the offer to me on the basis that "after all, a woman's personality changes once a month."

The only thing that had changed in 100 years, between these two happenings, were the members of the outgroup. The discrimination against me as a woman was as irrational as that against the Chinese. Menstruation was now deemed a factor limiting brainpower. The arguments were that the outgroups were already inept or corrupt thereby excusing the ingroup from trusting them, working with them or letting them, in their social or intellectual circle. It has been argued that the problem is not what constitutes the present makeup of the outgroup, but what fears the ingroup possesses.

> Research by Bettelheim and Janowitz (1964) indicated that the ultimate fear of prejudiced people is not that the status of the targeted population will change; rather, it is that *their* status will change as a result of a target population's advancement (Bryant, 1994, p. 24).

In the late 1800s, in another venue, the same argument against women was used as that used by the Toronto development company a century later. Throughout the United States, Canada, and Great Britain, there were heated debates as to whether a woman should receive higher education. In 1875, the Literary and Scientific Society of University College, The University of Toronto, debated: "Is it advisable that women receive a University or Professional Education?" In 1889, the Society voted to limit its membership to men only (Ford, 1985). Such debates presented little along the line of educational information, but much on attitudes about biology, particularly a woman's cycle. James MacGrigor Allan stated in an address to the London Anthropological Society, in 1869:

> At such times, women are unfit for any great mental or physical labour . . . In intellectual labour, man has surpassed, does now and always will surpass women, for the obvious reason that nature does not periodically interrupt his thought and application (Ford, 1985, p. 3).

In mentioning physical labor, it makes one wonder what these men thought of the women who worked side by side with their husbands on the Great Plains and Prairies of North America throughout that time. It is reminiscent of another time in history, that of Rosy the riveter. After World War II, the women who were so capable of working in munitions factories were relegated to the gentle suburbs, to keep in line with their capabilities.

It is always fascinating, and essential, to look behind the rhetoric and see the lifestyles that existed during the times of these prejudiced acts. Chinese labor was deemed crucial, particularly in building North American railroads. Women were deemed more controllable in the home. When those factors changed, the attitudes about those oppressed groups were commensurately altered also. Now, certain aspects of women and the Chinese are accepted, while other areas, such as total social acceptance and work opportunities, are still burdened with prejudice.

In my case, I would like to say that my pointing out to some of the men in the Toronto development company the illogical reasoning and blatant prejudice of their beliefs, words, and deeds made a difference. That was not so. What is frozen in my mind is their uniform expression of disbelief that someone they acknowledged to be intelligent could not grasp what they deemed to be a universal truth. I do know, however, my speaking out had two effects. First, it did force them to hear another view. Second, as painful as it was at the time, I now see that each time I stand up for what I believe to be right, it becomes easier for me to do the next time.

What struck me then, and what strikes me every time I read historical documents involving prejudice is the total lack of logic inherent in prejudice. Newman (1999) pointed out such examples.

> In the 1890s . . . the Irish and Italian Catholics, as well as Jews of Eastern European origin, were each considered separate races, distinct from Anglo-Saxon Protestants, and definitely not white. But by the mid-twentieth century, the descendents of these groups were assimilated as part of a newly defined white race and were reclassified 'Caucasians.' (p. 12)

Times had changed and the needs of the ingroup were different, necessitating an acceptance of former outgroups.

Cohen (1998) offered an additional explanation why, today, Ashkenazi Jews and recently arrived Asians and other "voluntary immigrants" are more accepted into the mainstream than African Americans. The former groups,

> . . . although leaving oppression behind, come in search of opportunity with positive motivation, so they focus especially hard, learn the system well, and often use schooling to get ahead. In contrast, involuntary or captive minorities, incorporated by conquest, or enslavement and exposed to subordination and discrimination for decades, see little hope of getting ahead and resist the mainstream culture. (p. 243)

This argument would hold true for Native North Americans, as well. But, the argument begs the question, why are Caucasians who "resist the mainstream culture" not discriminated against, and other groups who try to enter the mainstream not accepted? In addition to causing untold and unnecessary pain, racism continues to make a mockery of logic.

When we read historic documents, we marvel at what constituted prejudice at that time. There is often a smug sense of superiority to those who spoke with such assuredness at another time. For example, in 1911, the Senate Commission on Immigration reported that Poles are "darker than the Lithuanians" and "lighter than the average Russian" and that "Poles are more highly strung than their neighbors" (in Jacobson, 1998, p. 69). Today, it is difficult to see how any of that could be of any importance. What history shows us is the foolishness, at best, and the destructiveness, at worst, of holding onto prejudiced views. This begs the question, What are we holding onto today that, in short order, will be looked at smugly by those who read the history we make?

Where do we go from here?

Those who make prejudiced judgments about others, and they can be from the ingroup or outgroup, do not do so based on fact, but rather on what they think is required for personal happiness. In other words, as Cohen (1998) stated, "The inequality is in the ethnocentric eye of the beholder" (p. 61).

Does that mean that what always was, and is now, will always be? Maya Angelou, in the poem she wrote and read at President Bill Clinton's inauguration in 1993, listed some of the groups into which we have divided ourselves: the Asian, Hispanic, Jew, African American, Sioux, Catholic, Muslim, French, Greek, Irish, Rabbi, Sheik, Greek, Gay, Straight, Preacher, privileged, homeless, Teacher, Turk, Arab, Swede, German, Eskimo, Scot, Italian, Hungarian, Pole, Ashanti, Yoruba, and Kru. She then challenged us to look into each other's eyes and faces

And say simply
Very simply
With hope–
Good Morning. (pp. 4-6, 10)

There is no way to give a definitive answer as to when, or even whether, her words will come true. What is known is that there is a better chance for understanding between groups if three conditions exist. First, the more knowledgeable each individual is within each group about other groups, the less chance that person will resort to discrimination. That is not to say that the power of economics or political aspirations will not undo changes in attitudes and, consequently, changes in behavior. But, the more knowledgeable each individual is about the deleterious consequences of racism, both for the giver and the receiver, as witnessed throughout history, the better chance there will be that individuals will think twice before exhibiting such destructive behavior. And, in that moment of thinking twice, the human species has a chance to move one step toward acceptance, one step away from racist thought and behavior. This will always be accomplished by one more moment of understanding, by one individual at a time.

Second is what Pettigrew calls "the norm of human heartedness" (i.e. an inherent caring about another) found in "virtually all major religions and ethical traditions" and in the secular American penchant for "rooting for the underdog" (in Bryant, 1994, p. 6). This, too, will not annihilate prejudice. Rather, it is another tool to put the human species on the path of understanding and acceptance.

Third, there needs to be a greater awareness of the destructive effects of prejudice on the bigot. The spotlight is presently on the suffering of the oppressed who have endured everything from social exclusion to extermination. Their pain marches through the pages of history. Notwithstanding, victimizers, unbeknownst to themselves, make themselves victims. "What must not be forgotten is that ethnic prejudice has victims on both sides. Bigots are the victims of their upbringings, experiences, and social environments" (Bryant, 1994, p. 17). And they work hard to pass on these upbringings, experiences and prejudiced social environments. It affects how they deal with life. It is a burden they forever carry around with them, justifying why they do what they do. "Prejudice does not appear suddenly in a mind that is unprepared to accept it or spontaneously in the minds of a group of people" (Bryant, 1994, p. 20). Prejudice is something a person has to work at, and work at full time. It is something that blocks much that is good in life from the life of the bigot. In other words, no one can give pain without being mired in it.

There is always the question, But what can I do, I am only one person? Each one of us is one of the drops of water entering the hairline crack in the rock of prejudice. To illustrate our individual importance, I end with a personal story.

In the late 1970s, I was asked to cover a story for a small newspaper about a rabbi speaking at a Sunday church service to which members of his congregation were also invited. During the service, I noticed in a book, a prayer for the conversion of the Jews. At the luncheon/discussion following, I pointed out my finding. I was assured by the clergyman that the book was rarely used (the pages were still crisp) and the prayer never used. When the denomination had enough money, a new prayer book, excluding that prayer, would be published. I chose to write the story without that incident, arguing with the editor that if they didn't follow through with their promise, and the spirit of their promise, I would write about all. A later story of betrayal, on top of prejudice, I successfully argued, would be picked up by all major Canadian papers.

I let the church officials and congregants know my feelings. By also honoring their word, I gave them the opportunity, not only to change the prayer book, but also to continue their interfaith dialogue with the synagogue. They chose to do so.

The example of one person taking one step does not obliterate prejudice. It does, however, keep us on the path of lessening it by opening the hairline crack in the rock a bit more. It brings us closer to the day when we all will realize there are no races, other than the human race.

References

Angelou, M. (1993). **On the pulse of morning**. New York: Random House.

Bryant, B.K. (1994). **Counseling for racial understanding**. Alexandria, VA: American Counseling Association.

Cahill, T. (1998). **The gifts of the Jews: How a tribe of desert nomads changed the way everyone thinks and feels**. New York: Doubleday.

Cohen, M.N. (1998). **Culture of intolerance: Chauvinism, class, and racism in the United States**. New Haven: Yale University Press.

Ford, A.R. (1985). **A path not strewn with roses: One hundred years of women at The University Of Toronto 1884-1984**. Toronto: University of Toronto Press.

Jacobson, M.F. (1998). **Whiteness of a different color: European immigrants and the alchemy of race**. Cambridge, MA: Harvard university Press.

Newman, L.M. (1999). **White women's rights: The racial origins of feminism in the United States**. New York: Oxford University Press.

Weeks, J. (1995). **Invented moralities: Sexual values in an age of uncertainty**. New York: Columbia University Press.

CHAPTER 3
CONJECTURES OF A WHITE
ANGLO SAXON CATHOLIC FEMALE:
EXPERIENCES SHAPING MY CURRENT
ATTITUDE ABOUT RACISM

Mary Ann Jansen
The Union Institute
Cincinnati, Ohio

My neighborhood is changing. I don't think I like that. No one, I suppose, likes change. At present, as my neighborhood becomes more and more integrated, moving through varying degrees of economic status; changing its racial and cultural mix, moving from *white* to *black* and *Hispanic* and *Indian*; I find my sense of self changing. Change challenges the way that I fit. Change challenges me to change.

As I pump gas at the corner station, push my shopping cart through grocery aisles, or stand in line for my dry cleaning, at times I am acutely aware of the color of my skin. I'm more self-conscious of being *white*. Sometimes this doesn't bother me and yet at other times, surprisingly, I find an internal sense of inadequacy because I'm *white*. I know the history of oppression by my race toward other races. There are times, too, when the inadequacy moves to a fear. Why? Is it all about the possibility of eventually not belonging, of not being accepted? In the back of my mind I find thoughts to want to move from the neighborhood so as not to deal with change, not to face differences; but that is not who I am, this is not what I deeply want.

I don't claim to understand prejudice or racism. As a teacher, I've wrestled with the meaning of the two terms to bring my students to awareness and understanding. There have been few times that I personally have been the object of prejudice. There have been times when I've specifically had to confront my own prejudice, and now, with the evolution of my own neighborhood, it all comes into another focus.

I realize something more is being asked. Yes, it scares me, this change, but my background, my experiences, my beliefs in life call me to ask the question, How do I transform the fear so as to continue to create quality of life? What skills can I draw upon, what do I need further to learn? I am grateful that writing this chapter has brought me to greater awareness of my present life. I have recognized with more clarity the situation I am in now. I need to spend time naming, telling my experience.

What has brought me to the now in facing the fact that nothing stays the same, and the world is bigger than I ever dreamed? The world is knocking on my neighborhood door, and I trust it is knocking with opportunity. How do I know this? Because of what I have known.

I often draw upon an experience I had at 21. It made me aware of prejudice, the possibility of racism. I realized nothing is simple. Deep, deep issues are attached. Any time one's identity comes into play, a whole gamut of feelings and reactions unfold.

In 1974, I ventured to volunteer for a year on a Native American reservation in the west. Even as I remember today the experience, it is extremely painful. Before heading to South Dakota I never really had been exposed so intensely to another culture. I myself had never been a minority. In looking back I see that I *survived* the situation, that's how I would name it. I don't know if I would choose to do it again but the experience has been one of my greatest life learnings.

Naive, trusting, enthusiastic, belongings packed in a Toyota Celica with my 10 speed bike attached, I drove over 1,200 miles to find a world of pick up trucks, huge and rugged, suited for the Dakota plains far better than my tiny sports car. My 10 speed bike did no better in faring that western ruggedness. Within a short time, my tires were flat, attacked by huge burrs growing along the road. This was no place for a bike and I felt no place for me.

Like my tires, my enthusiasm and trust were deflated right away when, upon my arrival to the reservation, my hello to a group of passing teenagers, with whom I was to work, was answered with, "What do you think you're doing *honkie*?" I was stunned. How could they say this to me? Why would they say this to me? They didn't even know me.

I was soon to realize I was being greeted by centuries of experienced oppression, ingrained, festering in prejudice. In that one word, *honkie*, I was judged, valued, dismissed all within two minutes because of the color of my skin, not my person, not who I was as an individual. For them why should I be any different than any other *white*? This was the given at the beginning.

I suppose I was lucky that my response was tempered by shock. It would have been very easy to climb right back in the car and head home with a conditioned heart. It would have been so easy to close out the opportunity.

I struggled through months of isolation and alienation, as a volunteer at a Roman Catholic parish, to maintain my effort to spend time, to tell stories, and to build relationships. I'd often begin and end my day with the question, What am I doing? I had no real understanding of the skills it took to step into another culture. I had not been prepared, nor thought it necessary to learn about another culture. Weren't people basically the same? I had gumption, thanks to my experience growing up. It was a given that I liked people. I hung in there: my enthusiasm toned, my desire to learn fanned, my hope kept burning, dim at times but burning. My perseverance paid off.

My effort brought me to a day when two of my fourth grade students invited me to sled ride with their family one Sunday afternoon in January. That day of sled riding speaks volumes to me of what can happen in life. It was a moment of initiative, inclusion, acceptance.

I remember how the two dark faced boys concisely spoke the invitation. With eyes focused toward the floor (a behavior that I had first experienced as very threatening), they told me their family would be going out to sled ride that afternoon, would I come? Through the months I had recognized such lack of eye contact was a cultural practice and not a reaction to something I did; I realized that it was not my fault. Understanding saved me from possible feelings of disregard. Even though I had developed in my culture a need for eye contact, through understanding of Native American cultural ways, the boy's behavior did not bother me. I immediately said yes to their invitation, knowing the day was to be more than sled riding. I could not believe what was happening. I was offered a chance to be included beyond my professional role.

Some hours later, myself and others tightly bundled on top of an overturned car hood tied to the back of a pick-up by a sturdy rope, were being pulled at a good clip, through a biting wind, across the deep snow covered hills of the vast winter white plains. I was not aware at first but I was the only one present who was not Sioux. When I finally became aware, my internal joy equaled the exhilaration of the sled riding.

But strangely, accompanying this joy was an overwhelming fear-filled sense of awe. In being included, accepted, I sensed the awesomeness of this position. What was this greater responsibility that I was called to now that there was an opening for such relationship? I was now more than the tolerated white woman, no longer an object. I was entering more deeply a story that I would be asked in relationship to understand.

Such a relationship brought to light my foolishness when earlier in the year, I had tried to solve a deeply troubling issue through a simple naive step. Two Catholic churches existed in the South Dakota town, one *white* one *Indian*. The Indian church was designed and decorated just like the white one except it was the designated place of worship for the Native Americans–no more than four blocks separated the buildings. The question that had existed long before I had come to the Plains was what to do about the two buildings in such close proximity. Was it necessary that the priest have double the services each Sunday because of the two parishes? My solutions:

tear down both churches and build one, combine the congregations, thus eliminating so many scheduled Masses, but more so, move toward greater unity.

Being included on the sled ride with some 15 Sioux brought home a very deep awareness. I realized that there was much more to the church buildings than roof and windows and wood. The problem of the churches asked for more than a practical solution. The buildings contained stories, memories, centuries of culture, a living place to gather. What became obvious was that miles of history separated the two peoples. My simple choice for a solution would erase the concrete expressions of inherited life. My lack of sensitivity could eradicate what gives identity. Now that I had been invited to sled ride, now that I had been included, now that I moved a bit closer than the professional school teacher, I too saw individuals. Steps to uniting two peoples take more than construction of a building. Being invited to sled ride was not just an outing but a responsibility for me to explore who I was as a white, who these people were, each of them, as Native Americans. Relationship demands reflection.

I even began to ask myself what right I had in the decision making. I was the outsider serving in a role that allowed input on the decision. Because of my position in the *white* church working with the *Indian* church, because I, as a Caucasian person, had informal power established through the centuries, I could influence the life of these people. And how ironic that I was volunteering for only a year.

I've recently returned to that town where I spent not quite a year, yet much of my life. Since my time 25 years ago there I have studied the Sioux. When I returned, I found both churches still standing. The *Indian* church now offers in great detail Sioux heritage mingled with Christian theology. Brilliant Sioux designs border the ceiling and decorate the walls around windows. The Christ figure behind the altar, depicted as a great Sioux chief, wears buckskin and a headdress of colorful feathers. St. Joseph is the strong warrior. A statue of Kateri Tekawitha receives homage. Present, close to the tabernacle, is the leather pouch that contains the precious eagle feather. The church is alive in Sioux culture.

What a life lesson I have learned. Prejudice eradicated leads one not only to the responsibility of accepting the other but to grow in appreciation of all that the individual is, and to struggle to create an environment where the individual can truly live fully. Acceptance and appreciation evoke a challenge to balance the heritage and culture contained in the history of individuals. Story, story, story liberates; understanding unfolds, connections are made, relationships develop.

I do not struggle to make all the same but to recognize difference; to create *balance*. How important it is for myself as an individual to be secure for all this to happen. Yes, I am glad I found *two* churches on my return because I would want nothing to be destroyed. I am glad I can appreciate what the culture has to offer. Perhaps the history of the land made for the stronger story to be expressed. Perhaps as a white I am invited into that story, to celebrate it.

I do not know the answer for how to combine two histories. Will one church ever exist? All I know is that each individual holds so much in his/her story. In looking at my own story I know so much has gone into the making of my attitudes, experiences, and beliefs.

Differences, recognizing differences, naming differences, accepting differences, appreciating differences . . . what does it take, when does it begin? Where did it begin for me? How old was I: eight, nine, or maybe 11? I remember the toy truck, stretching 12 inches long from the front plastic bumper to the back door of its trailer. The cab, shiny black, trimmed with plastic chrome, had side doors that opened. Driving it from one end of the sidewalk to the other took our imaginations down highways across the country. Through the plastic windshield we could see the steering wheel and the seat where we sat controlling the rig; safely delivering the contents: twigs, empty match boxes, a toy car.

My playmate and I were children connected in creative play. I happened to be someone to play with for the day and he proved patient with me, the visiting tomboy. He lived in one of the 25 buildings of my sister's complex in Silver Spring, Maryland, outside Washington, DC. where I was staying for two weeks.

My sister's, a summer destination, was a 10 hour drive from my Midwest home. I saw her neighborhood different from my Cincinnati neighborhood only in that there were no houses, only long rectangle apartment buildings stretching across blacktopped parking lots. Address numbers on the doors and flower boxes or toys on the porches distinguished one apartment from the other, that and odd, strange smells wafting in the hallways. Such spices tantalizing my nose were not common in my life.

As I grew older, I came to know the apartment complex as a *United Nations*. The complex housed foreign government employees or others from around the globe, who worked in DC. Only years later did I realize how diverse this experience was.

To me, my playmate and I were no *different* except he owned the toy truck. Would my sister purchase one for me?

"Where did you get your truck?" I asked.

"Hanukkah."

Simple, I thought. That evening I asked my sister if sometime she would take me to look for a toy truck at a department store called *Hanukkah*.

Looking back I do not remember how I handled not receiving a toy truck from my sister, and I do not know when Hanukkah became something other than a department store, something other than Christmas. I grew up Catholic. During the first 13 years of my life everyone was basically Catholic from Santa Claus to every president of the United States, so I thought.

Not until my high school years in boarding school, and later, in my teaching profession did I realize that where I grew up, a very *safe* Catholic ghetto, was not the norm. In this *ghetto*, as all ghettos, practically everyone attended the same school, the same church, and seemed to think the same way with common goals and values.

Boarding school exposed me to students of varied economic and philosophical backgrounds as well as of different cultural backgrounds, particularly from Central and South America. New awarenesses were rich. What other meaning could "Reds" have than Cincinnati's beloved baseball team? A lot . . . and with Russia, no less! My time in boarding school gave me broadening perspectives and taught me skills for tolerance and acceptance. Living in as close proximity as a boarding school, 24 hours a day, could have been disastrous, but I learned to appreciate the story behind the differences, thus growing in appreciation of the individual(s).

In teaching, particularly the course, *The History of the American Roman Catholic Church*, I was surprised to learn that throughout history, my family as Irish-Catholic, experienced prejudice. The very date of March 17th, greatly celebrated in the streets and bars of the United States, had been a source of ridicule a century before.

Gradually did I realize growing up in the 1950s, the tables were turned in my small neighborhood from receiving prejudice to projecting prejudice. Only one Protestant family lived in our Cincinnati west-side neighborhood. My Irish/German Catholic mother tolerated that family. We could play with the Protestant children, but she indirectly communicated that they were different, not to be accepted in the same way as other neighbors. I know I internalized that something was wrong; that they, with what I interpreted as a *sickness,* were not as good as my Catholic neighbors. We tolerated the members of the Protestant family but they were people to keep at a distance. We were to feel sorry for them, which I realize now, gave us permission to be superior.

I learned that if others were different, I was then better than they. I could act on this attitude. Those who did not attend the Catholic parochial school were quietly ostracized, even those who were Catholic. There was no question which businesses or merchants would receive our business, only those run by Catholics. Life was easily and clearly defined in this context. I saw how I would fit into the world. I didn't have to work on tolerance; I just made those who were different second.

I can't help but wonder though, how my mother reconciled that she had a Protestant father who chose to take an Irish Catholic wife in the late 1800s. How was my grandmother accepted by his family, how did he allow his children to be raised Catholic? I've questioned this through the years, especially when I stand at my family's cemetery plot looking at the graves of my grandmother, aunts, and my uncle. Some distance away, buried in an unmarked grave, lies my grandfather, in the Protestant section of the Catholic cemetery. I am a product of a union between Protestant and Catholic. Do I claim the Protestant side?

I am left wondering about the boundaries we are given during childhood, boundaries arising from our heritage, boundaries that formed prejudice. When did it happen that I saw others as different? When did I learn to fight for those differences, when did I learn to let them go? Does one really let them go or does one just accept differences and learn to incorporate them in a larger boundary? As that child playing with the coveted truck I did not hesitate to interact with my Jewish playmate. I know it was in creative child's play that I, a Catholic, connected with a Jewish child. May I conclude that, initially, the human inclination is to relate; the drive to connect is greater than the need to keep separate?

I question as an adult when did I desire to let go of that part of my boundaries that separated me from others, excluded them? How am I learning to healthfully keep the identity those boundaries defined? How do I know the difference: what defines, what excludes? Is there a certain strength needed to even explore this question? Does one need to be grounded in who she is? I think so. I think it is imperative for an individual to possess a sense of security.

In my childhood I know I was given a sense of safety; I grew up in security. From that place of safety I was taught, even though there was unconscious prejudice, to reach out to others. I was given examples modeling compassion toward others. I had never known my mother to openly reject anyone. I never knew if our mailman was a Catholic, but I'd watch my mother greet him on our front porch on humid summer days with a cold glass of water. I listened as my mother, a nurse herself, often encouraged our *"colored" wash woman*, Ruth, to pursue nursing school. From the security of our home, I observed my mother safely reach out to individuals.

My father, a doctor, did not hesitate, like my mother, to help others. On the mornings I'd find my father absent from the breakfast table, I knew he had made a house call sometime during the night. And throughout my childhood, I partially comprehended stories of his hospital service in WWII in northern Africa. From these experiences of my father and my mother, I was taught a responsibility toward others. The effect of role modeling is beyond measurement.

Along with this sense of responsibility to others was communicated a sense of opportunity. Tunis, the Mediterranean, a toy camel, an Italian inlaid wood box with a secret compartment, all brought home from the war; *The Arabian Nights* for bedtime; fragments of my father's war stories began to weave in my psyche a mysterious world of people different, distant, dangerous, yet inviting. My father's language records of Russian, French, Italian, chosen, I'm sure for the list of American Allies, played in the background of my childhood. *Different* became enchanting. This proved true two doors down from my home where we, as children, were mesmerized listening to Mrs. Calis talk in a Greek accent as heavy as her short body. Each year we'd anticipate her Halloween hand out, the evening's favorite, feather light fried dough, laden with white sugar, which, at each bite, crumbled in our mouths and on our costumes.

Instilled with the intrigue of peoples of different cultures, with the excitement of foreign places, I developed a love of travel. I've followed that invitation to experience, to learn, across the Americas, to Europe; realizing on each return home how much richer my life is and, too, glad to be home. I focus much of my energy as a teacher arranging cultural trips for my students, creating processes that contribute to and build upon appreciation of the uniqueness and understanding of the other. There is no equal to learning outside the classroom walls.

As an educator, I face the challenge of how to develop in my students appreciation for the other. Observing my students on service learning field trips, especially to

Cherokee N.C. and Pine Ridge, South Dakota, has given me clues. I know people can share indirectly while working on common projects. Just like me and my Jewish playmate with the truck, human beings forget differences when focused in creative process. The creative process takes us beyond differences.

I have learned to design ways for stories to be told, either between individuals or about the heritage one is studying. I have learned the value of the council fire, the kitchen table, the college van for places to tell stories. Stories are so strong, forming a context that can hold differences, bring appreciation, and dissipate prejudice. I believe that by telling my story in this chapter I have greater awareness of my attitudes and greater freedom to accept others.

Create ways to enjoy together, as in the utter joy of sled riding. Create adventures where the creative can carry us and the human soul can rise up. My summers spent at my sister's apartment complex somehow provided me with experiences where differences translated into opportunities. Teach people to see the opportunity. And, I suppose, trust, hope, never give up; there are so many places to sled ride.

CHAPTER 4
RACISM: EARLY DEVELOPMENTAL
AND PSYCHOLOGICAL ASPECTS

Ronald Goldman
The Union Institute
Cincinnati, Ohio

P rogress toward alleviating racism is painfully slow. Perhaps a new approach is needed. The ideas offered here are not intended to replace, but rather to supplement other options and to expand our thinking about this seemingly intractable social problem.

We know how difficult it is to change existing racist attitudes. It is possible, and preferable, to prevent such attitudes from forming in the first place. Children are not inherently racist. However, sometime between birth and adolescence, children may exhibit racist attitudes and behaviors. We as adults are responsible. Adults control the social environment that teaches children to be racist. Psychologists understand the connection between early childhood experiences and later attitudes and personality structure. A central thesis of this chapter is that racism is a symptom of a much deeper and broader problem: adult attitudes and behavior toward children in general and infants in particular.

Behavior toward others is a reflection of one's feeling about oneself. Prejudice is more likely to occur among people who are insecure, lack self-esteem, and have reduced empathy. The following discussion describes how these factors are associated with how we view infants, the quality of the mother-child relationship, and various cultural child-rearing practices.

Rather than accepting or rejecting the ideas that follow, I invite you to hold open the possibility. The fact is that we do not know the validity of these ideas, yet we must ask the questions before they can begin to be answered. In order to encourage research, there must be plausibility in the questions. Accordingly, I have attempted to make the case for plausibility.

Before continuing, it may be helpful to clarify a few points of logic and meaning so that there will be no misunderstandings.

1. A statement that certain factors contribute to behavior or social condition X means only that this relationship is a possibility. *It is a speculation, not a conclusion.* Though the possibility may be perceived to be small, it remains a possibility, particularly when there has been no pertinent study to suggest otherwise.

2. The speculative statement (or question) about the possible effect of certain factors *does not exclude the presence of other possible factors that may contribute to X.*

3. The fact that in the majority of individual cases certain factors do not lead to *X does not refute the speculative statement.* For example, if a factor increases the incidence of X from 1 in 100 to 2 in 100, then the speculative statement is supported (and in this example, the change is significant) even though in the vast majority of individual cases, X does not occur as a result of the factor.

Attitudes Toward Infants

The typical attitude toward infants was perhaps illustrated by an incident a father related to me concerning his two-and-a-half-year-old son. He asked his son to put the milk in the refrigerator. After his son did this, the father for the first time thought, "He's a real person. My son is a real person!" Evidently, it was both his son's understanding of language and his ability to perform a customary physical act that led the father to this realization, but what about the first two and a half years of his son's life? Apparently, he had not previously been considered to be a "real person." People might say he was "just a baby." It is convenient not to consider the infant a person who has feelings. Then parents have license to do what they want with the infant.

Are we prejudiced when it comes to infants? Perceived differences are used to justify prejudice. We assume that when things look different, they are different. In comparing a newborn infant to an adult, we find many apparent differences: age, size, skin color, vocal and body language, intelligence, responsiveness, eating habits, body proportions, physical coordination and strength, interests, and personality, to name a few. Consequently, we tend to view infants as being very different from ourselves, and our attitudes and behavior can demonstrate our prejudice.

Despite the differences, infants are real people. When we deny an infant's humanity, we deny our own humanity. Our prejudiced view of infants says more about us than it does about them. The perceived differences are used to justify adult ethnocentrism, a view that adults are superior to non-adults. Our prejudice serves to conceal our own feelings of inferiority and low self-esteem (Stephan, Ageyev, & Coates-Shrider, 1994). Thus, we are part of a self-perpetuating cycle. We experience prejudice as infants when we are subjected to it by adults. When we become adults, we view infants (and other apparently dissimilar groups) with prejudice. We pass on to others what we ourselves have experienced.

We also falsely attribute our own feelings or traits to infants, an act called projection. For example, the belief that infants don't remember is a projection of our failure to remember our own infancy. Infants do remember, but the memories are generally unconscious in adults (Squire, 1986). If we think infants don't feel, it is a projection of our own lack of feeling. When we are not open to infant signals, we assume that infants do not communicate. Therefore, before evaluating the abilities of infants, we might first conduct some self-examination.

Researchers' understanding of the human infant has undergone a revolutionary change in the last 20 years because of innovative studies (Bower, 1989). They are learning how to design experiments that give infants an opportunity to teach us who they are. As a result, we are discovering that infants are much more capable than we ever thought possible. Even though infants are relatively helpless, without verbal language, and totally dependent on adults for their well-being, they are much like us, and they feel deeply both physically and emotionally. The latest research on infant development confirms that human infants are very aware, sensitive, perceptive, and responsive to their environment. All senses are working, and infants seek sensory stimulation. Purposeful movement has been observed within minutes of birth. Facial expressions are similar to those of adults. Smiling has been observed at birth. Cries are meaningful and can express specific feelings and needs.

The behavior of infants is rational, and they are enthusiastic learners. Infants have specific preferences, and they can even evaluate their experience. Their memory and learning abilities have been demonstrated from various behavioral experiments and physiological responses. Their ability to learn a given behavior and respond to obtain a reward suggests mental activity and anticipation. The more we discover about infants, the more we discover about ourselves. There is great potential that as we learn and implement what we learn, we can give the next generation a much better start in life.

Recognizing the infant as a person has important implications, not the least of which is recognizing infant autonomy. Infants have preferences, wants, and needs. Adults can choose to dismiss many of these because of the overwhelming physical power and control they have over the infant. Such adult behavior teaches the infant that one must have physical power to get what one wants or needs. But if adults instead recognize the infant as a person, there is a relationship to consider. Ignoring the infant's needs solely because one has greater physical power and control weakens the relationship, because the infant's feelings do matter.

Perhaps dehumanizing infants, being insensitive to their needs and abilities, subjecting them to prejudice, and denying their autonomy contributes to such attitudes directed toward other minority groups in adults.

Mother-Child Relationship

The mother-infant relationship is a primary relationship. Although the infant's relationship with the father and others is important, the quality of this principal relationship has profound long-term consequences. A strong bond between mother and infant contributes to the child's mental and social development. The infant-mother relationship is a model for infant-peer relationships (Bowlby, 1960). In addition, research demonstrates that securely attached infants are more curious and sociable with peers at two, three, and five years of age. The child's self-confidence and empathy are also connected with the quality of the relationship with the mother (Arend, Gove, & Sroufe, 1979). Attachment affects the body as well as the behavior. Securely attached infants are more physiologically in tune with their mothers, and they have improved immune functioning and lowered stress levels (Donovan & Leavitt, 1985).

Many factors can disrupt the mother-child bond. For example, it can be disrupted by mother-child separation (including separations resulting from hospital policies). Numerous studies of monkeys have demonstrated that maternal-infant separation causes significantly more stress (as measured by the level of stress hormone cortisol in the blood) in the infant than in the mother, that even a 30 minute separation is highly stressful for the infant, that high stress can be present despite a lack of crying, that infant contact with other monkeys during the separation does not relieve this stress, and that the effects of separation can last long after reunion with the mother (Vogt & Levine, 1980). Furthermore, it has been shown that human infants and children and monkey infants have similar behavioral and physiological responses to maternal separation (Laudenslager, 1988). Investigators have found that the response of young children to separation has two phases: protest followed by despair. Other responses include helplessness, hypervigilance, withdrawal, depressed activity level and heart rate, higher stress level, and suppressed immune response (Hollenbeck et al., 1980). In addition to separation, childhood maltreatment and trauma are also connected with poor attachment (Youngblade & Belsky, 1989).

Disrupted bonding is common in American infant care and child rearing. For example, although it is widely accepted that optimum care for an infant requires almost constant contact with the mother (Blurton-Jones, 1972), this level of caretaking is not typical in America. Not only are the mother and infant often separated in the hospital after birth, but half of all infants have mothers who work outside the home (Clarke-Stewart, 1989). By contrast, in a hunter-gatherer society, the infant is in contact with the mother 70-80% of the time during the first year and the rest of the time with someone else (Konner, 1976). Extensive nonmaternal care of infants in the first year is associated with insecure infant-mother attachment (Belsky, 1988). Could the developmental changes associated with these cultural practices contribute to the formation of personality structures that are prone to racism and other anti-social attitudes and behaviors?

Reduced Self-Esteem and Empathy

Early experience and the mother-infant relationship may affect self-esteem. Low self-esteem has both personal and social consequences. Those with low self-esteem generally have a low opinion of others, a fundamental component of racism (Allport, 1954). Low self-esteem is also associated with relationship dissatisfaction, poorer general health, depression, drug use, and loneliness (Nelson, Hill-Barlow, & Benedict, 1994). None of these associated factors would contribute to respect and concern for the feelings of others. In an attempt to compensate for their low self-esteem, some people may adopt certain behaviors.

Generally, males try to restore their self-esteem by competing and telling themselves they are bigger or better than others. If they don't believe it on a personal level, they may become attached to a group that fulfills that requirement, whether it is a sports team, social club, or other association. As psychologist Gordon Allport (1954) stated, "The easiest idea to sell anyone is that he is better than someone else" (p. 372). The connection between low self-esteem and racism is obvious.

Empathy is the universal human ability to experience the same emotions that someone else is experiencing. Newborn infants cry when they hear other newborn infants crying (Hoffman, 1981). This is an empathetic response to the distress of another. With empathy we acknowledge, "I feel like you. I am like you." Despite the obvious differences, adults and infants are alike in fundamental ways. Both are human beings who need love and human contact. Both can experience a wide spectrum of emotions, including feeling hurt or angry when needs are not met.

Empathy is the key to following the golden rule. When we feel empathy, we feel connected to others and treat them well. Without empathy we are separate and are more likely to mistreat others. Clearly, racism and empathy are incompatible and inversely related.

A child's natural empathy is either nurtured or inhibited by environmental influences. Inflicting trauma on a child results in a reduced ability to empathize. For example, toddlers who were abused expressed no concern for crying peers and even attacked them (Main & George, 1985).

A Potential Factor Connected With Reduced Empathy,
Low Self-Esteem, and Disrupted Bonding

Imagine that you are resting comfortably, perhaps with a loved one you enjoy being physically close to, when a few strange people enter the room and proceed to pick you up to carry you away. You ask what this is about, and get no answer. You protest and struggle, but they are stronger than you are. They take you to another room where they remove your clothes and strap you down on your back on a table. You try to free yourself, but the only part of your body that you can move is your head. All this time they continue to disregard your protest. Then a man enters, and after seeing that you are secure, he picks up a knife and starts to cut off a piece of skin from your genitals. The procedure lasts for about fifteen minutes. Your screams of pain are ignored. How do you feel?

There is no question that such an experience would be intolerable. It is likely that it would result in trauma. Psychologists have long known that trauma has long-term effects on one's inner life, as well as on social behavior and functioning. One important characteristic of trauma is that the precipitating event, along with connections to current symptoms and behaviors, is often hidden from awareness.

From the perspective of the one being restrained and cut, the above-imagined scene is similar to an infant's circumcision. How does being circumcised feel to the infant? Anatomical, neurochemical, physiological, and behavioral studies confirm that newborn responses to pain are "similar to but greater than those in adult subjects" (Anand & Hickey, 1987). Infants circumcised without anesthesia (reflecting common practice) experienced not only severe pain, but also an increased risk of choking and difficulty breathing (Lander, Brady-Fryer, Metcalfe, Nazarali, & Muttitt, 1997). Increases in heart rate of 55 beats per minute have been recorded, about a 50% increase over the baseline (Benini, Johnson, Faucher, & Aranda, 1993). After circumcision, the level of blood cortisol (stress hormone) increased by a factor of three to four times the level prior to circumcision (Gunnar, Malone, Vance, & Fisch, 1985). As a surgical procedure, circumcision has been described as "among the most painful performed in neonatal medicine." (Ryan & Finer, 1994). Investigators reported, "This level of pain would not be tolerated by older patients (Williamson & Williamson, 1983). Using a pacifier during circumcision reduced crying but did not affect hormonal pain response (Gunnar, Fisch, & Malone, 1984). An infant also may go into a state of shock to escape the overwhelming pain (Romberg, 1985). Therefore, while crying may be absent, other body signals demonstrate that severe pain is always present during circumcision. (This discussion may raise various questions about the practice of circumcision for the reader. For more information, see contact information at the end of this chapter.)

Behavioral changes in infants resulting from circumcision are very common and can interfere with parent-infant bonding and feeding (Anand & Hickey, 1987). The American Academy of Pediatrics Task Force on Circumcision notes increased irritability, varying sleep patterns, and changes in infant-maternal interaction after circumcision (American Academy of Pediatrics, 1989). In one of the most important studies, the behavior of nearly 90% of circumcised infants significantly changed after the circumcision. Some became irritable and others were withdrawn. In addition, the researchers observed that circumcised infants had lessened ability to comfort themselves or to be comforted by others. This change could interfere with the mother-child relationship.

Canadian investigators report that during vaccinations at age four to six months, circumcised boys had increased behavioral pain response and cried for significantly longer periods than did intact boys. The authors believe that circumcision may induce long-lasting changes in infant pain behavior (Taddio, Katz, Ilersich, & Koren, 1997). This study suggested that circumcision may permanently alter the structure and function of developing neural pathways (Walco, Cassidy, & Schechter, 1994).

An infant's survival depends on adult empathy. Crying, together with associated facial and body movement, is all the infant has to communicate distress to the caretaker. When no one responds to the infant's cries of distress, he gets the message that nobody cares about his feelings and that he is powerless and terrifyingly alone. Such is the experience of the circumcised infant. This lack of empathetic response is related to the limited ability of some adults to feel. If we do not have empathy for infants, they may not have empathy for others. Perhaps this is why circumcised men have such difficulty empathizing with circumcised infants.

Circumcision may also affect self-esteem because it results in a significant loss for males. Taylor, Lockwood, and Taylor (1996) studied the foreskin tissue at the Department of Pathology, Health Sciences Centre, University of Manitoba, Canada. They reported their results in the **British Journal of Urology** in an article titled "*The Prepuce: Specialized Mucosa of the Penis and Its Loss to Circumcision.*" Based on the examination of 22 adult foreskins obtained at autopsy, they found that the outer foreskin's concentration of nerves is "impressive" and its "sensitivity to light touch and pain are similar to that of the skin of the penis as a whole" (p. 294). The foreskin inner surface is different. It is mucous membrane similar to the inner surface of the mouth, also rich in nerves and blood vessels. Between the inner and outer layers of the foreskin is a unique structure they call a "ridged band" that contains "specialized nerve endings" (p. 294). The researchers conclude that the foreskin has several kinds of nerves and "should be considered a structural and functional unit made up of more or less specialized parts . . . The glans and penile shaft gain excellently if surrogate sensitivity from the prepuce" (p. 295).

The foreskin represents at least a third of the penile skin. It protects the glans from abrasion and contact with clothes (Ritter, 1992). The foreskin also increases sexual pleasure by sliding up and down on the shaft, stimulating the glans by alternately covering and exposing it. This can occur during masturbation or intercourse. Friction is minimized, and supplementary lubrication is not needed (Bigelow, 1995). Without the foreskin, the glans skin, which is normally moist mucous membrane, becomes dry and thickens considerably in response to continued exposure. This change reduces its sensitivity (Ritter, 1992). In addition, the loss of a secretion called smegma of the inner foreskin layer removes natural lubrication.

Only men circumcised as adults can experience the difference a foreskin makes. In the **Journal of Sex Research**, Money and Davison (1983) from the Johns Hopkins University School of Medicine reported on five such men. Changes included diminished penile sensitivity and less penile gratification. The investigators concluded:

> Erotosexually and cosmetically, the operation is, for the most part, contraindicated, and it should be evaluated in terms of possible pathological sequelae. (p. 291)

Though men may be unaware of the effects of circumcision, the fear that their penis is somehow deficient is reported to be widespread in our culture (Toussieng, 1977). Commercial interests have responded to this concern. A 1995 issue of a popular national men's magazine contained 10 advertisements for penile enlargement by various methods. (The American Urological Association concludes that they are not safe and effective.) One full-page ad proclaimed, "No man ever needs to feel inadequate again." Another asked, "Isn't it time to feel better about yourself?" Male preoccupation with the penis is also reflected in a survey of what men think women find attractive in men. The data showed that men greatly exaggerated the importance of penis size as a physical attribute that attracts women (Gagnon, 1977).

An aspect of oneself can be identified with a particular body part, as masculinity is typically identified with the penis. When that part is wounded, there often is a corresponding psychic wound to the self, a loss of self-esteem. Fifty percent of respondents to a survey of self-selected circumcised men reported low self-esteem as a harmful effect of their circumcision (Hammond, 1999). We do not know how much circumcision may contribute to reduced empathy, low self-esteem, and disrupted bonding, all factors that could be associated with racist attitudes.

Circumcision As Trauma

If trauma results in reduced empathy, the relationship between circumcision and trauma deserves attention. Studies investigating circumcision pain have referred to circumcision as traumatic (Taddio et al., 1997). The **Diagnostic and Statistical Manual of Mental Disorders (DSM-IV)** published by the American Psychiatric Association (1994) is helpful in discussing the question of trauma as it relates to circumcision. Its description of a traumatic event includes an event that is beyond usual human experience, such as assault (sexual or physical), torture, and a threat to one's physical integrity. An assault is a physical attack. Torture is severe pain or anguish. It does not necessarily take account of intention or purpose but focuses on the act itself and the experience of the victim.

From the perspective of the infant, all the elements in this **DSM-IV** *description* of traumatic events apply to circumcision of a male infant: the procedure involves being forcibly restrained, having part of the penis cut off, and experiencing extreme pain. Based on the nature of the experience and considering the extreme physiological and behavioral responses of the infant, circumcision traumatizes the infant.

The question of an infant's capacity to experience trauma needs to be emphasized. John Wilson, an author with a national reputation for trauma research, supports the view that effects of trauma can occur "at any point in the life cycle, from infancy and childhood to the waning years of life" (Wilson, 1989). In addition, the **DSM-IV** states that traumatic effects "can occur at any age" (p. 426).

Conclusion

Culturally "normal" infant care and treatment can traumatize a child and contribute to poor self-esteem, disrupted bonding, and reduced empathy–factors that may be associated with racist behavior. Much of what is done in hospitals to newborn infants violates maternal instincts. When we fail to trust and act on our impulses, we forfeit our personal power and become victims of our own fear. Parents need to be aware of the impact of their choices and make them prudently. In some cases, protecting the best interests of their child may require that the parents make an extra effort to verify questionable information, and the result may be a decision that goes against "standard practice."

Decisions that deviate from the norm are not usually easy to make. Conclusions that secure attachment requires that the mother have close contact with the child may seem obvious to some, but these conclusions challenge the beliefs and lifestyle of others. Cultural change will be required in order to support optimum infant care. Public education on the importance of secure attachment is needed because if the bonding does not happen, the infant will suffer, whether that suffering is actively expressed or not. Similar comments apply to the harmful practice of male circumcision.

The idea of infant autonomy conflicts with most parents' beliefs, but isn't it the parents' inherent responsibility to care for the infant, which includes satisfying the infant's needs? Generally, most parents were not given this kind of care when they were children. Parents face the challenge of examining what they believe about child rearing and how they choose to treat their children instead of simply enforcing their will with their power. If we want our children to treat others with respect and consideration, whatever their physical or social standing, then we need to treat our children that way from birth.

Proper understanding, appreciation, and care of infants, along with increased awareness and resolution of our own childhood pain, may help to alleviate not just racism, but numerous other social problems. The change starts with questioning our attitudes toward infants, learning about them, and sharing our wisdom and intuition with those who will be raising the next generation. If we trust children more and the "experts" less, we can transform our society.

References

Allport, G. (1954). **The nature of prejudice**. Cambridge, MA: Addison-Wesley.

American Academy of Pediatrics. (1989). *Report of the task force on circumcision*. **Pediatrics**, *84*, 388-391.

American Psychiatric Association. (1994). **Diagnostic and statistical manual of mental disorders** (4th ed.) Washington, DC: Author.

Anand, K., & Hickey, P. (1987). *Pain and its effects in the human neonate and fetus*. **New England Journal of Medicine**, *317*, 1321-1329.

Arend, R., Gove, F., & Sroufe, L. (1979). *Continuity of individual adaptation from infancy to kindergarten: A predictive study of ego-resiliency and curiosity in preschoolers*. **Child Development**, *50*, 950-959.

Belsky, J. (1988). *Infant day care and socio-emotional development: The United States*. **Journal of Child Psychology and Psychiatry and Allied Disciplines**, *29*, 397-406.

Benini, F., Johnson, C., Faucher, D., & Aranda, J. (1993). *Topical anesthesia during circumcision in newborn infants*. **Journal of the American Medical Association**, *270*, 850-853.

Bigelow, J. (1995). **The joy of uncircumcising**. Aptos, CA: Hourglass.

Blurton-Jones, N. (1972). *Comparative aspects of mother child contact*. In N. Blurton Jones (Ed.), **Ethological studies of child behavior**. New York: Cambridge University Press.

Bower, T. (1989). **The rational infant**. New York: Freeman.

Bowlby, J. (1960). *Grief and mourning in infancy and early childhood*. **Psychoanalytic Study of the Child**, *15*, 9-52.

Clarke-Stewart, K. (1989). *Infant day care: Maligned or malignant?* **American Psychologist**, *44*, 266-273.

Donovan, W., & Leavitt, L. (1985). *Physiological assessment of mother-infant attachment*. **Journal of the American Academy of Child Psychiatry**, 24, 65-70.

Gagnon, J. (Ed.). (1977). **Human sexuality in today's world**. Boston: Little & Brown.

Gunnar, M., Fisch, R., & Malone, S. (1984). *The effects of a pacifying stimulus on behavioral and adrenocortical responses to circumcision in the newborn*. **Journal of the American Academy of Child Psychiatry**, 23, 34-38.

Gunnar, M., Malone, S., Vance, G., & Fisch, R. (1985). *Coping with aversive stimulation in the neonatal period: Quiet sleep and plasma cortisol levels during recovery from circumcision*. **Child Development**, *56*, 824-834.

Hammond, T. (1999). *A preliminary poll of men circumcised in infancy or childhood*. **BJU International**, *83*, 85-92.

Hoffman, M. (1981). *Is altruism part of human nature?* **Journal of Personality and Social Psychology**, *40*, 121-137.

Hollenbeck, A., et al. (1980). *Children with serious illness: Behavioral correlates of separation and isolation*. **Child Psychiatry and Human Development**, *11*, 3-11.

Konner, M. (1976). *Maternal care, infant behavior, and development among the Kung*. In R. Lee & I. Devotes (Eds.), **Kalahari hunter gathers**. Cambridge, MA: Harvard University Press.

Lander, J., Brady-Fryer, M., Metcalfe, J., Nazarali, S., & Muttitt, S. (1997). *Comparison of ring block, dorsal penile nerve block, and topical anesthesia for neonatal circumcision.* **Journal of the American Medical Association,** *278,* 2157-2162.

Laudenslager, M. (1988). *The psychobiology of loss: Lessons from human and nonhuman primates.* **Journal of Social Issues,** *44,* 19-36.

Main, M., & George, C. (1985). *Responses of abused and disadvantaged toddlers to distress in agemates: A study in the daycare setting.* **Developmental Psychology,** *21,* 407-412.

Money, J., & Davison, J. (1983). *Adult penile circumcision: Erotosexual and cosmetic sequelae.* **Journal of Sex Research,** *19,* 291.

Nelson, E., Hill-Barlow, D., & Benedict, J. (1994). *Addiction versus intimacy as related to sexual involvement in a relationship.* **Journal of Sex and Marital Therapy,** *20,* 35-45.

Ritter, T. (1992). **Say no to circumcision.** Aptos, CA: Hourglass.

Romberg, R. (1985). **Circumcision: The painful dilemma.** South Hadley, MA: Bergin & Garvey.

Ryan, C., & Finer, N. (1994). *Changing attitudes and practices regarding local analgesia for newborn circumcision.* **Pediatrics,** *94,* 232.

Squire, L. (1986). *Mechanisms of memory.* **Science,** *232,* 1612-1619.

Stephan, W., Ageyev, V., & Coates-Shrider, L. (1994). *On the relationship between stereotypes and prejudice: An international study.* **Personality and Social Psychology Bulletin,** *20,* 277-284.

Taddio, A., Katz, J., Ilersich, A., & Koren, G. (1997). *Effect of neonatal circumcision on pain response during subsequent routine vaccination.* **The Lancet,** *349,* 599-603.

Taylor, J., Lockwood, A., & Taylor, A. (1996). *The prepuce: Specialized mucosa of the penis and its loss to circumcision.* **British Journal of Urology,** *77,* 294.

Toussieng, P. (1977). *Men's fear of having too small a penis.* **Medical Aspects of Human Sexuality,** *11,* 62-70.

Vogt, J., & Levine, S. (1980). *Response of mother and infant squirrel monkeys to separation and disturbance.* **Physiology and Behavior,** *24,* 829-832.

Walco, G., Cassidy, R., & Schechter, N. (1994). *Pain, hurt, and harm.* **New England Journal of Medicine,** *331,* 542.

Williamson, P., & Williamson, M. (1983). *Physiologic stress reduction by a local anesthetic during newborn circumcision.* **Pediatrics,** *71,* 40.

Wilson, J. (1989). **Trauma, transformation, and healing.** New York: Brunner/Mazel.

Youngblade, L., & Belsky, J. (1989). *Child maltreatment, infant-parent attachment security, and dysfunctional peer relationships in toddlerhood.* **Topics in Early Childhood Special Education,** 9, 1-15.

CHAPTER 5
THE CONTENT OF HER CHARACTER

Janet Avery
The Union Institute
Cincinnati, Ohio

T he Reverend Dr. Calvin Butts described Gloria Turner as a gift during the invocation at her memorial service on June 23, 1999. This is a fitting description for someone who had a profound effect on the lives of many people.

Gloria Turner was a vice president at one of the most prestigious financial institutions in the world, and used her influence to help people, especially members of the African American race, of which she was extremely proud to be a part. She was responsible for grant-making in the areas of health, housing, community revitalization, and economic development in New York City. In addition, she facilitated corporate funding for employment training for adults. She also served on a variety of nonprofit advisory committees throughout New York City.

I met Gloria in January, 1995, when she came to our organization on a site visit to determine whether or not her company would award us a grant. She made a lasting impression on me, and we later became friends.

One day while we were having lunch, she told me why she worked so hard to prove herself and why it was important to her that African Americans know that each one of us had to push ourselves in order to move forward as a people. She was extremely passionate about her desire to share this information. At the time, I was writing an article for a monthly publication and thought that it would be great to write an article about her. I never did complete the project. However, after her memorial service, I was asked to submit a chapter for this book and I believed this would be a good opportunity for me to attempt to put her passion on paper.

Everyone with whom I spoke enjoyed recounting their relationship with Gloria and what she meant to them. She wanted her life to add value to the lives of others, and there is no doubt that it did. She was a woman on a mission. Though only five feet four inches tall, she had a powerful presence. She conducted a one-woman crusade to stamp out the limiting impact of racism. One of her goals was to educate people so that they would respect themselves and others. Gloria felt it was imperative that African Americans find a source of pride that was not tainted by slavery. In an effort to promote this pride, she studied African history and made several trips to Africa so that she could share her new learning with people she could educate and encourage. Her mother said that she had been a giving person since she was a child. She would often bring home children who did not have the same support system that she possessed.

An admirer of Gloria, who worked in her department, said,

> Although I am not an African American, Gloria inspired me. She made me think. As a result of her consciousness raising conversations, I was encouraged to think about how I would be if my history were dominated by oppression. She also made me proud of the fact that the major reason that I work at a prestigious institution is because I work hard and am willing to put forth the effort to succeed. Gloria made me aware of the fact that when an individual can override circumstances and succeed, in spite of the obstacles, this person weakens the impact of racism.

When asked how Gloria viewed or defined racism, her relatives, colleagues, and friends were not at a loss for words. All of the comments expressed the fact that Gloria had no patience for pettiness and ignorance. Some of the comments were: "Gloria thought racism was poison, poison that went down into the soil and caused everything to rot; Racism didn't exist for Gloria and since it didn't exist, she didn't validate it or allow herself or anyone around her to be crippled or limited by it; Gloria believed that racism meant that one was not given equal opportunities." Her views mirrored those expressed in **The Alchemy of Race and Rights**, by Patricia J. Williams (1991):

> What is truly demeaning in this era of double-speak-no-evil is going on interviews and not getting hired because someone doesn't think we'll be comfortable. It is demeaning not to get promoted because we're judged "too weak," then putting in a lot of energy the next time and getting fired because we're "too strong." It is demeaning to be told what we find demeaning. It is very demeaning to stand on street corners unemployed and begging. It is downright demeaning to have to explain why we haven't been employed for months and then watch the job go to someone who is "more experienced." It is outrageously demeaning that none of this can be called racism, even if it happens only to, or to large numbers of, black people; as long as it's done with a smile, a handshake, and a shrug; as long as the phantom-word "race" is never used. (pp. 48-49)

Although the above quote may have been characteristic of Gloria's description of racism, there were no "phantom words" which she felt uncomfortable using with a person of any persuasion. In fact, it was her honesty and candor that allowed her to be effective in slicing through the silence that often allows racism to thrive. Her courage (which was expressed by almost everyone with whom I spoke) prompted others to speak boldly.

One of her colleagues and dear friends, a Caucasian man (who visited her faithfully until her death and spoke at her funeral in Virginia), looked at me with eyes filled with tears and said, "One of the things that I loved most about Gloria was that she cared less about appropriateness than truth. She spoke what was on her mind and heart regardless of with whom she was speaking. Although she was loving and polite, she called it like it was."

As evidenced by her speech and actions: Its clear that Gloria Turner has learned from listening to her gut feeling, that inner voice that tells her to seize hold of opportunities. "You don't get anywhere by always playing safe," remarks Gloria. "You have to be willing to make a stretch, take on the difficult challenges. If you don't, how will you ever know what you're capable of?"

Another business associate, a Caucasian woman, had grown to love Gloria and was instrumental in arranging her memorial service. She told me that Gloria shared her thoughts about injustices that some Caucasian colleagues had imposed upon her. This woman said that Gloria was not angry or hostile and had no chip on her shoulder. She was simply stating her belief. I asked her how she felt. She said that she appreciated the fact that Gloria had the courage to tell her. The same person told me that when she was purchasing a new home in a neighborhood that had a 25% African American residency, which was increasing, Gloria spent time telling her about what often happens to the value of property when the percentage of African American residency increases. She cared about her colleague and wanted to make sure that she made an informed decision. This woman told me that she appreciated candidly and constructively discussing the "white flight" issue with an African American.

Gloria was a complex woman. She spoke the truth, not to harm or injure, but to help. She was not mean-spirited, bigoted, or vindictive. Her goal was to cause people to see that injustices existed and to do what they could, from their place in the world, to improve the imbalance brought about as a result of ignorance, which was one of her definitions of racism. Listening to Gloria speak is reminiscent of William Hazlitt, British essayist, who said, "Prejudice is the child of ignorance."

While interviewing Gloria's friends and relatives to ascertain whether she had the same impact that I thought she might have in causing them to be more candid and verbal about issues regarding race, it occurred to me that one's definition of an injustice greatly influences how one chooses to solve the problem. For example, someone might read the following text and become defensive, angry, and/or hostile:

> Both quantitative and qualitative evidence suggest that blacks continue to be discriminated against in employment. Furthermore, their relative labor market status has clearly declined in the past 10 to 20 years as labor demand has ap-

parently shifted away from less educated workers in general and away from less educated blacks in particular.

Gloria, however, would have focused on the fact that something must be done to address this issue.

Since Gloria believed that racism resulted in diminished opportunities, she sought to alleviate those wrongs by creating or opening up opportunities for people she felt were targets. One of her dear friends said, "She lifted people up. She educated people so that they were willing to see things from a different perspective." Gloria accomplished her mission by making non-African Americans aware of the consequences of racism and by educating African Americans about their responsibility to help themselves and not wait for others to open doors for them.

She was a role model to others with respect to working hard in order to succeed in life. At age 35, she left her job at Philip Morris and returned to college. Two years later, she graduated and obtained a job, at the company where she would become a vice president, as an operations management trainee.

Gloria pushed herself to grow. She had no qualms about telling young and old African Americans alike how their behaviors and mannerisms were keeping them from progressing personally and professionally. Although it was not a formal part of her job description, she took it upon herself to serve as a mentor to newly hired young African Americans. Several of her colleagues said that before the organization had a diversity initiative, Gloria was a one-woman diversity program. She was instrumental in shepherding new people who came to the firm so that they would not feel lost and out of place. Two of her colleagues gave me a collection of "do's and don't's" that she distributed to young professionals so that they would be aware of what habits and behaviors would help or hinder their performance and progress. The package contained information regarding table manners, a corporate survival checklist, and the importance of proper speech.

I'll never forget the day that I met Gloria. She came to our organization on a site visit to determine whether or not her company would approve a funding proposal that we had submitted. At this point in my career, I had met with many funders and thought that I was prepared for almost any question that someone might ask. Little did I know that the person who would interview me would be Gloria Turner. She asked the usual polite questions. Then she looked at me, as only Gloria could look at you, and said, "You are clearly doing good work; why is your budget so small? Why don't you have more funders?"

I had always considered myself a direct, no-nonsense person. It was clear I had more than met my match. After asking the questions, she looked at (or should I say through) me and waited for my answer. After what seemed like an eternity, I knew that I had better tell her the truth or she would cut me to ribbons. So, embarrassed and frightened, I told her that I felt strange asking for money. I felt like I was begging. She told me that was a poor excuse and that if I wanted to be successful in my job, I'd better figure out how to get comfortable fundraising. Then she told me that she wasn't going to be an advocate for my obtaining funding from her company if I couldn't do it for myself. She said that she did not want to attend the funding meeting and appear as if she was just supporting me because I was another African American woman. "Do a better job of fundraising, and I'll recommend that we fund you," she told me. After I peeled myself off the floor, I looked at her in total disbelief and said, "Thank you for your honesty." She said, "You're welcome," smiled, and left.

She was determined to make the path to professional success easier for her niece and nephew, whom she dearly loved, than it had been for her. She provided them with private tutoring, SAT training, and trips to Africa.

Excellence was a way of life for her, and she accepted nothing less from herself or others. A dear friend of hers said that each year they would go on vacation and share their personal goals. Gloria's goals usually revolved around professional growth and how she would use her advancement to help people who needed knowledge and guidance. She believed that she could make the world a better place by making a positive contribution in the lives of others. Gloria's life is a good illustration of the following statement from Booker T. Washington (1901):

> In my contact with people I find that, as a rule, it is only the little, narrow people who live for themselves, who never read good books, who do not travel, who never open up their souls in a way to permit them to come into contact with other souls; with the great outside world. No man whose vision is bounded by color can come into contact with what is highest and best in the world. In meeting men, in many places, I have found that the happiest people are those who do the most for others; the most miserable are those who do the least. I have also found that few things, if any, are capable of making one so blind and narrow as race prejudice. I often say to our students in the course of my talks to them on Sunday evenings in the chapel, that the longer I live and the more experience I have of the world, the more I am convinced that, after all, the one thing that is most worth living for; and dying for if need be, is the opportunity of making someone else more happy and more useful. (pp. 228-229)

One could see the contribution that Gloria made toward alleviating racism by looking at those in attendance at her memorial service. Abyssinian Baptist Church in New York City was filled with what looked like an international convention. Toward the end of the service, one of the ministers suggested that each person hug a neighbor. It was evident that the feisty Gloria Turner, who spoke with truth and candor about racial injustices, had convinced people to move beyond the rhetoric of racial politeness to touch others in a meaningful way.

As stated by a dear friend at the service, "The one thing that she did not get to do was to write her book." Gloria did not have an opportunity to leave the legacy of a book. She did, however, leave a chapter in the heart of each of the people whose lives she touched.

References

Washington, B.T. (1901). **Up from slavery**. New York: Penguin Books.
Williams, P.J. (1991). **The alchemy of race and rights**. Cambridge, MA: Harvard University Press.

CHAPTER 6
UNDERSTANDING YOUR CHRISTIAN STUDENTS' ATTITUDES TOWARD RACISM: DOES TRAINING IN THE CHRISTIAN RELIGION CAUSE RACIAL PREJUDICE?

Jeff Garrett
Glenn Doston
Ohio University
Athens, Ohio

Does Training in the Christian Religion Cause Racial Prejudice?

Is there a relationship between racism and Christianity? Since Jesus taught believers to live by the law of love (Matthew 22:36-40) and the Golden Rule (Matthew 7:12), one might assume that Christians are not prejudiced. *Yet social scientists have consistently found that people who are more religious are more bigoted.* Eleazer (1950) believed that prejudice grows out of six elements; ethnocentrism, faulty assumptions, groundless fears, group conflict, cultural lag, and fallacious teaching. Apparently, there are Christians who are finding this in the churches that they attend. Brighan and Weissbach (1972) found that church-goers tend to be more prejudice than non-church-goers. Thirty-five years ago, Kelsey (1965) suggested that churches are the most segregated institution in society. Things haven't changed much. In most areas of the country, the most segregated time of the week is Sunday morning.

The Chicago Theological Seminary (1968) documented a history of racism in Christianity. No one can deny the harm that has been inflicted on humanity in the name of Jesus Christ. Batson (1976) wrote,

> Espousing the highest good, seeking to make all men brothers [and all women sisters], religion has produced the Crusades, the Inquisition, and an unending series of witch hunts. Virtually every organized religion has been the excuse, if not the cause, for violent, inhumane, and antisocial acts. (p. 30)

Kirkpatrick (1993) found that Christian fundamentalism was positively related to all measures of discriminatory attitudes. Rokeach (1970) wrote,

> Most disturbing are findings that show that the religiously devout are on the average more bigoted, more authoritarian, more dogmatic, and more anti-humanitarian than the less devout. Such findings are disturbing from a religious standpoint because they point to a social institution that needs to be reformed. They are disturbing from an anti-religious standpoint because they point to a social institution that deserves to be destroyed. (p. 33)

The research is clear, on the average Christians are more bigoted than non-Christians. Gorsuch and Aleshire (1974) write,

> When church membership is the only measure of religious commitment, the results are clear and consistent. Church members are more prejudiced than those who have never joined a church. All of the studies found the same relationship, which was statistically significant when tested. (p. 289)

How can we understand this paradox? How can it be that a group of people who are taught to love everyone and live by the Golden Rule be more prejudiced? Does training in the Christian religion actually cause prejudice? What is the true relationship between religion and racism? The source of prejudice is not religion. The key to understanding the relationship between religion and racism is to assess one's approach, or orientation, religion.

Religious Orientation

There are at least six different orientations that one can take toward religion. Each of the orientations differs with respect to tolerance and prejudice. First, extrinsically motivated religious people tend to be more prejudiced. Individuals whose orientation is extrinsic use religion as a means to another end; such as security, comfort, status, social support for themselves (Allport & Ross, 1967). Faith in Christ and devotion to his teaching are not what these individuals value. Their religion is no value in its own right; religion is merely a utilitarian function to meet self-centered needs. That is why prejudice is very compatible with an extrinsic orientation toward religion. In his article, *"Gimme the Old Time Racism,"* Brannon (1970) wrote, "Prejudice and instrumental [his term for 'extrinsic'] religion both satisfy the same psychological needs. . . . Both prejudice and religion can be crutches for a weak ego" (p. 43). Extrinsically motivated religious individuals do a good job giving organized religion a bad name.

Second, intrinsically motivated religious individuals, on the other hand are less prejudiced. They view their faith as an end in itself. Allport and Ross (1967) wrote,

> It [religion] is not a mere mode of conformity, or a crutch or a tranquilizer or a bid for status. All needs are subordinated to an overarching religious commitment. In internalizing the total creed of his [or her] religion the individual necessarily internalizes its values of humility, compassion, and love of neighbor. In such a life (where religion is an intrinsic and dominant value) there is no place for rejection, contempt or condescension towards [other people]. (p. 441)

Allport and Ross (1967) summarized the distinction between these first two orientations by saying, "The extrinsically motivated person *uses* his [or her] religion, whereas the intrinsically motivated *lives* his [or her] religion" (p. 434).

Third, individuals who are indiscriminately pro-religious are *for* religion in general. Allport and Ross (1967) identified this orientation because there were some individuals who endorsed both intrinsic and extrinsic items on their instrument that measures religious orientation. Individuals with this orientation are not committed to any creed but they are pro-religion. Allport found that these people were highly prejudiced.

Fourth, indiscriminately anti-religious individuals are *against* anything that has to do with organized religion (Allport & Ross, 1967). There is not much that we can conclude about the prejudiced attitudes of this group, other than they may be less tolerant of people involved in organized religion. Further research needs to be done before any conclusions are drawn.

The fifth orientation is non-religious. This orientation is comprised of individuals who are not *for* or *against* religion, they simply don't practice religion. Gorsuch and Aleshire (1974) said that "The highly committed religious person is–*along with the non-religious person*–one of the least prejudiced members in our society." Thus, the non-religious, along with the intrinsically motivated religious person, tend to be less prejudiced than the extrinsically motivated or the pro-religious.

The sixth and final orientation toward religion is quest (Batson, 1976). Batson (1976) stated that people with a quest orientation toward religion are "not necessarily aligned with a formal religious institution or creed . . . [they] are continually raising ultimate 'whys,' both about the existing social structure and about the structure of life itself" (p. 32). Individuals with a quest orientation are preoccupied with existential issues, questioning the complexities of life. In short, the quest orientation tends to be less dogmatic, less prejudiced and more responsive to the needs of others. Batson's claims that only those with a quest orientation realize a genuine reduction in prejudice. However, Donahue (1985) noted that Batson's studies were based on small samples (average N = 50). Another limitation is that all of his studies were performed on college students from Preston and the outcomes of his studies may not be generalizable to church members across the country. Nevertheless, Batson has made an important contribution with the quest orientation as an alternative to Allport's I-E model.

Fundamentalism And Christian Orthodoxy

Two other important dimensions, which help us understand the true relationship between religion and racism, are fundamentalism and Christian orthodoxy. Kirkpatrick (1993) suggested that fundamentalism is a stronger predictor of prejudiced than Allport's dimension of extrinsic.

Some researchers view fundamentalism and Christian orthodoxy as one in the same (Herek, 1987), but we (along with Kirkpatrick, 1993; Gorsuch, & Aleshire 1974; Hunsberger, 1995) view fundamentalism and Christian Orthodoxy as two distinct constructs, not alternative synonyms for a single dimension. One can be Orthodox in one's Christian beliefs and not be a fundamentalist. In the literature, Fundamentalism is usually associated with religious sectarianism, religious dogmatism, and religious hostility (Glock & Stark, 1966, Hunsberger, 1995; Kirkpatrick, 1993). Fundamentalism has less to do with content and more to do with attitude or mindset. A fundamentalist typically has an authoritarian personality, a closed belief system, and is highly prejudiced.

Christian orthodoxy, on the other had has more to do with content and less to do with attitude or mindset. Glock and Stark (1966) and Fullerton and Hunsberger (1982) have developed a scale to assess Christian orthodoxy as distinct from fundamentalism. Fullerton and Hunsberger (1982) claimed that their scale assesses "the acceptance of well-defined, central tenets of the Christian religion . . . [including items] on which [there] is virtually unanimous consent by Catholics and Protestants alike" (p. 318).

The terms fundamentalism and Christian Orthodoxy should not be used interchangeably for two reasons. First, Hunsberger (1995) stated that there is a strong bias against fundamentalism (especially in other world religions) in the media and elsewhere. Journalist Almas Alam (as in Hunsberger, 1993) pointed out that "Fundamentalism [has become] a dirty word. . . . It is used pejoratively and is taken to imply bigotry, ruthlessness, hatred and a commitment to terrorism and militancy" (p. 113). Hunsberger goes on to explain that his conceptualization of fundamentalism makes no assumptions about bigotry, ruthlessness, and hatred. In some academic circles, however, the term "Christian fundamentalism" is associated with bigotry and the term is often used in a pejorative way. Thus, the first reason fundamentalism should not be used interchangeably with Christian Orthodoxy is that the term fundamentalism connotes a negative, prejudiced attitude.

The second and most important reason one should not confuse the terms has already been demonstrated in that they are two separate dimensions. The items on the DOS assess the content of a belief system, not the attitude of the believer. Fundamentalism, on the other hand, has more to do with the attitude of the believer. Empirical research demonstrates that Christian Orthodoxy and fundamentalism are distinctly unique (Hunsberger, 1995). The Christian with orthodox beliefs can hold their convictions in such a way that they are less prejudiced and are willing to question, and even doubt, (John 20:27, 28; Jude 22) their most cherished beliefs. This openness to change and grow in their spiritual development stands in direct contrast to the closed minded fundamentalist.

Conclusions and Implications

Knowing the differences between the six religious orientations, in addition to the dimensions of fundamentalism and orthodoxy, allows educators to understand the worldview of their Christian students. There are five major conclusions we can make regarding the research that we have reviewed.

1. On the average, church members are more bigoted than non members.
2. This overall finding, if taken only by itself obscures a curvilinear relationship (an inverted U). Allport and Ross (1967) wrote, "While it is true that most church members are *more* prejudiced than non-members, a significant minority of them are *less* prejudiced" (p. 432). In Donahue's (1985) meta-analysis, the curvilinear relationship was consistent in all empirical research on the subject of religion and prejudice.
3. Extrinsic and pro-religious orientations are both high in prejudice.
4. Intrinsic and quest orientations are both low in prejudice.
5. Future research will need to be conducted before making conclusions regarding anti-religious and non-religious orientations.

Educators should avoid making broad general statements about Christians being prejudiced. Allport and Ross (1967) wrote

To build a theory without noting the curvilinear relationship means that one would need to group together those who are high in prejudice with those who are low in prejudice. It would also imply that the more religious one is, the more prejudiced one is even though empirical findings are counter to this hypothesis. Such simplistic theories could also lead to conclusions that the source of prejudice lies within the religious institution and their teaching. But this explanation is rather difficult to accept because research demonstrates that religiously active are among the least prejudiced people–not the most." (p. 441)

It is virtually impossible to teach without encountering Christians. In Golnick and Chinn's (1996) text, "Multicultural Education in a Pluralistic Society," they listed religious groups in the United States. There are 100 Buddhist Temples in the United States with 100,000 members. There are 3,416 synagogues with 4,057,339 members of the Jewish Faith. But the overwhelming majority of religious people in the United States are Christian. There are 23,000 Roman Catholic churches in the United States with 57,019,948 members. There are 320,039 Protestant churches with 79,386,506 members. Almost half of the U.S. population claims to have faith in Jesus Christ.

In view of the inevitability that educators will have Christians in their classes, what should be a teacher's attitude toward their Christian students? Educators who assume that all Christians are highly prejudiced may be reluctant to even admit Christians into their graduate programs. John Gartner (1986) conducted a study focusing on anti-religious prejudice in admissions to doctoral programs in Clinical Psychology. A mock application to graduate school was mailed to professors of clinical psychology, and he found that psychology professors are reluctant to admit conservative religious applicants into their graduate school–which is a violation of the APA code of Ethics and the Law.

Teachers and professors need to examine their own attitudes, because religious discrimination is just as wrong as any other form of discrimination. It may help anti-religious educators to remember that many Christian churches played an important role in the Civil Rights Movement. Martin Luther King Jr. is an excellent example of an intrinsically motivated Christian who inspired many Christians to be activists. From behind prison bars King wrote:

> In the midst of a mighty struggle to rid our nation of racial and economic injustice I have heard many ministers say, "Those are social issues with which the gospel has no real concern." And I have watched many churches commit themselves to a completely otherworldly religion which makes a strange, unbiblical distinction between body and soul, between the sacred and the secular. . . . But the judgment of God is upon the church as never before. If today's church does not recapture the sacrificial spirit of the early church it will lose its authenticity, forfeit the loyalty of millions, and be dismissed as an irrelevant social club with no meaning for the 20th century. (Findlay, 1990, pp. 69-70)

A fundamental principle of multiculturalism is to understand the worldview of the people you serve. In his text "Counseling the Culturally Different," D.W. Sue (1990), described the characteristics of a culturally skilled counselor. The authors of this chapter have borrowed from Sue's list and adapted it to five characteristics of an effective multicultural educator:

1. Be aware of your own values and biases and how they may affect your students (i.e., if you are pro-religious or anti-religious your attitude will affect the people you serve).
2. Be comfortable with the differences that exist between you and your students in terms of religious beliefs.

3. Be sensitive to circumstances (such as personal bias or lack of knowledge) that may dictate referral of the student to someone who is competent.
4. Acquire specific knowledge and information about the particular group (in the chapter it is conservative Christians) you are working with.
5. Develop a good understanding of the sociopolitical system's operation in the United States with respect to its treatment of religious groups.

The information in this chapter is important regardless of your religious orientation. You may be Jewish, atheist, agnostic, Buddhist, Hindu, Muslim, Unitarian, Spiritualist or whatever other faith there is; regardless, you can grow to possess the five characteristics of an effective multicultural educator.

Imagine

If You Will . . . If we could at this very moment shrink the earth's population to a village with a population of exactly 100, and all existing human ratios remained the same, it would look like this:

- *57 Asians*
- *21 Europeans*
- *14 North, Central, and South Americans*
- *8 Africans*

- *70 would be non-white, 30 white*
- *70 non-Christian, 30 Christian*
- *50% of the entire village's wealth would be in the hands of six people, and all six would be citizens of the United States*
- *70 would be unable to read*
- *50 would suffer from malnutrition*
- *80 would live in sub-standard housing*
- *1 out of 100 would have a university education*

One wonders, if I lived in this small global village, how might the others' environmental and developmental concerns affect me?

(Reprinted – Carol Hanson with the assistance of data provided by the U.N. Demographic Data Division).

References

Allport, G., & Ross, M.J. (1967). *Personal religious orientation and prejudice.* **Journal of Personality and Social Psychology,** *5*(4), 432-443.
Batson, D.A. (1976). *Religion as prosocial: Agent or double agent.* **Journal for the Scientific Study of Religion,** *15*(1), 29-45.

Brannon, R.C. (1970). *Gimme that old time racism*. **Psychology Today**, *3*, 42-44.

Brighan, J.C., & Weissbach, T.A. (Eds.). (1972). **Racial attitudes in America**. New York: Harper and Row.

Donahue, M.J. (1985). *Intrinsic and extrinsic religiousness: Review and meta-analysis*. **Journal of Personality and Social Psychology**, *48*(2), 400-419.

Eleazer, R.B. (1950). **Reason, religion and race**. New York: Abengdon-Cokesbury.

Findlay, J.F. (1990, June). *Religion and politics in the sixties: The churches and civil rights act of 1964*. **The Journal of American History**, 67-92.

Fullerton, J.T., & Hunsberger, B.E. (1982). *A uni-dimensional measure of Christian orthodoxy*. **Journal for the Scientific Study of Religion**, *21*, 317-326.

Glock, C.Y., & Stark, R. (1966). **Christian beliefs and anti-semitism**. New York: Harper and Row.

Gartner, J.D. (1986). *Antireligious prejudice in admissions to doctoral programs in clinical psychology*. **Professional Psychology Research and Practice**, *17*(5), 473-475.

Golnick, D.M., & Chinn, P.C. (1994). **Multicultural education in a pluralistic society**. New York: Macmillan College Publishing Company, Inc.

Gorsuch, R.L., & Aleshire, D. (1974). *Christian faith and ethnic prejudice: A review and interpretation of research*. **Journal for the Scientific Study of Religion**, *13*, 281-307.

Herek, G.M. (1987). *Religious orientation and prejudice: A comparison of racial and sexual attitudes*. **Personality and Social Psychology Bulletin**, *13*(1), 34-44.

Hunsberger, B. (1995). *Religion and prejudice: The role of religious fundamentalism, quest, and right-wing authoritarianism*. **Journal of Social Issues**, *51*(2), 113-129.

Kirkpatrick, L.A. (1993). *Fundamentalism, Christian orthodoxy, and religious orientation as predictors of discriminatory attitudes*. **Journal of the Scientific Study of Religion**, *1993*(3), 256-268.

Kelsey, G.D. (1965). **Racism and the Christian understanding of man**. New York: Charles Schribner's Sons.

Rokeach, M. (1970). Faith, hope and bigotry. **Psychology Today**, *3*, 33-37.

Students of Chicago Theological Seminary. (1968). **Racism and white Christians**. Chicago: Chicago Theological Seminary.

CHAPTER 7
BEYOND RACISM:
AN INTERNATIONAL PERSPECTIVE

W. Henry Alderfer
Lauren Alderfer
New Dalai, India

What is racism? How does racism manifest itself? Racism, as defined in **The American Heritage Dictionary** (1989), is "the theory that there is a causal link between inherited physical traits and certain traits of personality, intellect, or culture arid, combined with it, the notion that some races are inherently superior to others." Are these traits prevalent in cultures around the globe? Does racism manifest in similar ways in different cultures? Are common manifestations of racism found in very distinct countries and cultures? Below, an international perspective will be given, highlighting personal observations from three unique countries: Ecuador, El Salvador and India. Insights into socioeconomic factors, ethnicity, economic power and domination, skin color, and caste will be exemplified through personal anecdotes, based on over 20 years of living and working outside our native America. Lastly, through the example of three contemporary world leaders, basic human values needed to get beyond racism will be proposed.

Ecuador

Ecuador is a small Andean country that straddles the equator in South America. Holed by a landed aristocracy of mostly Hispanic descent, nearly 50% of its population is Indian; another 40% is Mestizo (Indian and Spanish blood), less than 1% is Caucasian, and a small portion of the population is black or Mulatto. A constant coming and going of Indians, Mestizos, and Caucasians was a common sight to our children throughout their young lives. A sense of equanimity, or perhaps indifference, to one's ethnicity or skin color seemed to pervade their understanding of the world. We had a rude awakening one day when our elder daughter, at the age of six, returned home from a bus ride with her Ecuadorian godmother. She was confused and upset, questioning why the Indians had been pushed to the back of the bus and been treated so unkindly by the Mestizos. Clearly, this was an innocent child's observation of the greater society in which she lived. In fact, through her pristine eyes, she crystallized one of the major forms of racism in Ecuador: ethnic superiority.

El Salvador

El Salvador is the smallest of the seven Central American republics, and lies on the Pacific Ocean. Before the Spanish arrival, El Salvador was populated by five Indian tribes of Aztec and Mayan origin. Today, El Salvador is comprised of 94% Mestizo (Indian and Spanish blood), 5% Indian and 1% Caucasian. Amazing as it may seem, until recently the constitution discouraged blacks from living in El Salvador, and one rarely sees any blacks, even in the cosmopolitan capital city of San Salvador where over one million people live.

El Salvador and the United States have close ties. Most of the Salvadorans who left their country for the United States were poor, uneducated, and brown-skinned. They left, in most cases, because of socioeconomic discrimination at home, where their country is dominated politically and economically by what is commonly referred to as the "14 families of El Salvador."

One of the local schools, where most of the 14 families sent their children, began an exchange program with its sister school in suburban Washington, DC. The first group of Salvadoran students was a group from the high school. Upon their return to El Salvador, the students expressed a new appreciation for their country. They were very positive and enthusiastic for having learned about their own country from a new perspective; namely, from that of the Salvadorans who had immigrated to the United States. The school administration was very pleased with the cultural exchange and the newfound cultural understanding the high school students had gained. The school leaders were surprised when they faced great parental concern about the cultural environment where their children had their home stays. When the second group of Salvadoran students prepared for another student exchange the following year, the school administrators were careful to make specific selections of "American" home stay families based on color and economic status to avoid parental displeasure, and to ensure continued support of the exchange program. The parents' blatant unwillingness to cross color boundaries for their children, even during a two-week exchange program, clearly exemplified both the fear of the parents to expose their children to other racial groups and the socioeconomic conditions they considered inferior to their own. The common perspective of many of these parents was that we live on an island of prosperity and racial unanimity, which we will guard and protect for our children: we must protect our status gun.

India

India is one of the largest countries in the world. Its population of nearly one billion is second only to China. India has one of the oldest civilizations on earth. It is the birthplace of many religions including: Hinduism, Buddhism, Zorastrianism, Jainism. Language (of which there are 16 major cries spoken) and caste, rather than ethnic origin, are the primary distinguishing characteristics of the Indian population. Even though the caste system is now officially outlawed, and has decreased some- what in importance since Mahatma Gandhi's anti-caste movement during the mid-20th century, caste more than culture or creed, is still what defines modern India, particularly for the lower and middle classes. Caste remains one of the primary de- termining factors of one's future, hopes, and dreams. If the parent is a tailor, me- chanic, clothes washer, or sweeper, chances are the child will be the same. To further propagate this situation, marriages are normally arranged around economic and caste lines; those who stray from the norm are ostracized and ridiculed.

Although caste is one of the most important socioeconomic determinants in In- dia, skin color is also an important factor. Most lower castes are also of darker skin color, and if other sociocultural factors are equal, then the darker one's skin color, the more inferior–socially and economically–one is considered.

During Diwali, one of the most important festivities of the year, rituals such us lighting candles at an altar and praying before the altar to pay respects to the deities are performed. The entire staff participated in this ritual at the office. We wanted the "sweeper" to join. In India, there are two kinds of sweepers: one who sweeps inside, the other who sweets outside and is not allowed inside the house. We invited the outside office sweeper in, a cultural norm we easily broke as foreigners. At first, the sweeper would not come in; however, out of respect to the gods, or feeling obligated to the boss, with bowed head and stooped body, she reluctantly agreed. She quickly lit the religious candles. Then she proceeded toward us. Never taking her eyes off the ground, she dropped to her knees, kissed our feet, and quickly took leave. We were stunned and taken aback with a flood of emotion. As Americans, we initially felt pity for what we thought was such a demeaning act. Upon further reflection, we grace- fully accepted her act as one of respect and honor (traditionally reserved for saints!). Yet, upon still further analysis, this spontaneous act, done with utmost humility, epitomized the sweeper's self-perception, her sense of self-worth, and her awareness of her "place" in society. This simple vignette illustrated the greater undertone of racial and caste inferiority deeply rooted in Indian culture.

Beyond Racism

What are some of the common causes of racism as exemplified in these personal anecdotes remembered from three distinct cultures? Was ethnicity the major cause? Was the determining factor socioeconomic? Was skin color the predominant factor? As exemplified in the soon American attitude toward the downtrodden Indian culture and ethnic heritage, ethnicity played a major role. Socioeconomic dominance of one group over another was highlighted particularly in the example from Central America; however, in all three cases, the lower group in the socioeconomic stratum was the victim of prejudice. Color was exemplified in each culture: the group with the darker skin color was treated unfairly.

It would be too simplistic to pinpoint any one factor and claim that this factor alone is the cause of racism. Racism is an extremely complex phenomenon with a myriad of causes; and it is prevalent, we would assert, in most cultures of the world. Recognizing racism's pervasive and intrinsic nature in most culture is the first step toward overcoming it in our own lives and in the countries in which we live. Secondly, we need to realize that the manifestations of racism stem from the desire to remain powerful, dominant, and superior to our fellow humans. Yet in a world which is quickly becoming smaller and more interdependent, and which cannot survive in equilibrium if the rich become richer and the poor poorer, we must commit ourselves, our families, and communities to affirmative action to change and overcome racism.

Dr. Martin Luther King, Jr. proved that non-violence is a powerful and effective tool for social change to overcome racism. This same concept known as "ahimsa," (or non violence towards all living creatures) as professed by Mahtma Gandhi, asks each person to feel the interconnectedness and interdependence of the world in which we live. They urged people the world over to understand that we are all brothers, and that our souls are the same in the eyes of God; both King and Gandhi set examples of racial respect, tolerance, and human equality.

The 1909 Nobel peace laureate, Tenzin Gyatan, His Holiness the fourteenth Dalai Lama, is a living example of one who has gone beyond racism. Since the Chinese occupation of Tibet in 1950, the Dalai Lama, the spiritual and political leader of the Tibetan government-in-exile, has seen the devastation of his culture, the assassination of tens of thousands of his people, and the torture of countless others. He has not raised up the sword of justice to right the wrongs against his people, rather he says, ". . . peace has a chance to exist only when the atmosphere is congenial. We must first create that atmosphere. In order to do that, we must adopt the right attitude" (Ocean of Wisdom, 1981, p. 959). His exemplary life of compassion, love and respect, dignity and equality for all peoples and cultures has changed the daily lives of millions. On a global level, it has amalgamated the world community behind a "Free" Tibet through non-violence and passive resistance. On an individual level, he asks people to change their own attitudes and "to cultivate and develop genuine compassion" (Words In Harmony, 1990) within ourselves.

Racism and its corollary, domination, subjugation, and superiority of one people over another are rampant in the world today. We as individuals often feel powerless to change this situation. However, it is with us as individuals that the change must begin. We need to look at our own lives and see if there are any vestiges of racism in our minds and hearts, and root them out. As we have seen in the anecdotal examples of day-to-day life events in three cultures described in this chapter, at times racism pervades our innermost thoughts and simple outward activity, without us even knowing it; or if we do know it, reacting to it as if it were an acceptable norm of society.

We must change ourselves first, as King, Gandhi, and the Dalai Lama have done, and then we can transform our families, friends, and community. Our personal examples will form the body politic which will change the destiny of nations and humankind's core belief and value system, freeing us from the violence, hatred, and intolerance that racism breeds. Therefore, let us begin with a right attitude and embody the ideals of equality, respect, tolerance, compassion, and dignity of all peoples to get beyond racism.

References

The American heritage dictionary. (1981). Boston: Houghton Mifflin Company.

Ocean of wisdom, p. 64. (1981). Santa Fe, NM: The Dalai Lama, Clear Light Publishers.

Worlds in Harmony, H.H., p. 134. (1996). Delhi, India: The Dalai Lama, by arrangement with Parallaz Press, USA, Full Circle.

CHAPTER 8
THE LIFE EXPERIENCES THAT SHAPED YOUR CURRENT ATTITUDE ABOUT RACISM

Amelia Gross
The Union Institute
Cincinnati, Ohio

As I reflect upon my life experiences about attitudes toward racism, I find my mind swimming with various perceptions, life lessons, and consequences that have shaped my current thinking as it pertains to the topic of diversity. As a child growing up, my biological parents, both immigrants from the Ukraine and Poland, raised me. I was born after a year of my parents arrived in this great country, America. It took both my parents a number of years to master the English language and become familiar with the American lifestyle that represented freedom on all fronts, or so it seemed. It was for this reason that they migrated to this country. In an effort to change their previously strained living conditions, they looked at America as a place to develop a happy and secure home. Nevertheless, like anywhere they were met with a number of discriminatory situations. Although they were considered the "white" working class, this did not shield them from the constant reminder that they were foreigners, almost guests, in this country. It is interesting looking back at this attitude, since this great country was a melting pot of immigrants. How quickly that was forgotten as our country expanded and flourished.

My parents raised me with a strong work ethic and an attitude of being color-blind. The only real discrimination I experienced under their guidance was that of being lazy. They had little or no tolerance for that, unless you were ill for one reason or another. Unless mental illness was obvious, there was no excuse for not becoming a strong, independent person within your own right. I was, however, raised in a working class environment that was predominately white. I rarely, if ever, saw people of color except in the field of maintenance when my mother took me shopping. I remember one of my first encounters was that of a black woman as a ladies room attendant in an elegant department store known as Wanamakers in Philadelphia. I can still see my mother instructing me to use the facility with respect and cleanliness, so as not to burden this woman with any disrespect for her job. I was told she is not my maid under any conditions and I should treat her as any woman doing her job. My mother made her deposit of some coins at that time into the woman's tip jar as a token of our appreciation for her attention. However, I remember another group of women who came in and threw paper around and looked at this woman as if she did not exist, or better yet, was there to service them regardless of the mess they left. This became a valuable lesson I learned at the age of around four.

I also recall seeing a little black girl in the park situated across the street from our row house at that time. I found myself mesmerized by the braids in her hair. How I envied this little girl, after all I had poker-straight fine hair, which my mother would painstakingly curl each evening in pins. I assumed that they grew out of her head that way (I was quite young, I might add). As I grew older, I finally asked the other girl how she maintained this incredible crown of artwork. She proceeded to explain how her mother would take the time necessary to create the perfect rows of symmetrical braids with the addition of beads of her favorite colors. She also proceeded to explain that she wished she had my hair, because she loved curls and envied the ease with which they fell. It was then that our differences were just that, "differences" in texture and not as human beings. I befriended her and we played regularly at the park, swinging, chanting, and playing jump rope. There was no color, just warmth between two friends. Ah, if we could only capture our innocence from youth and carry it throughout our lives, but some forget, or better yet, do not take the time to remember.

At that time people of color were referred to as "colored people." I saw this on TV and remember neighbors addressing them as such. I am 45 years old at this time and it is amazing the various transitions of names given to people of color. I can remember some of the nastier people calling them Niggers, which never quite seemed right even at a young age. Then, as time went on, they were addressed as black, African Americans, and at this point "people of color" seems to be the most accepted. I can also recall no difference between the Latino population. If one's skin was darker and not naturally tan, one was "colored." The rest of the white population was considered either rich or poor by many accounts. I guess we were somewhere in between. I can remember boarding the bus to go into the city. The bus driver on a number of occasions was black. He seemed okay to most white people because "he wore a uniform," I could hear them say.

I held a position in the Pentagon when I was 20 years of age, and I have tried to remember my perceptions on racism at that time. The only real thought was that of the race relations classes we were made to attend. I still, for the life of me, cannot remember what I was supposed to absorb from these summers. I recall something about the fact that we were not allowed to discriminate. Since this did not affect my position, I can only imagine that the seminars were not very potent in promoting awareness since no one ever talked about them when completed. After two years in the Pentagon, I married and worked in Germany. My husband was an officer. My recollection during that time was very vivid–many, many race relations classes. I remember thinking there must be something going on since this was mandatory on a regular basis. However, I still failed to see the strength in their agenda. Looking back, I can only imagine that this was an effort to promote equality. I do not remember much racism at that time, maybe because we were in a foreign country and all looked at one another as Americans. Although I do recall the black officers, I never saw such a polished looking group of men. They definitely were more polished than most white officers I saw, and in better shape from working out. In retrospect, I can only imagine how they felt in that they had to work much harder, look much better, and out perform all the others. A tough weight to pull. They did it, and did it well. They certainly were men to make our country proud.

I also got my first glimpse of interracial marriages. This was most obvious among the enlisted men since most arrived single. A number of them married German women. Almost each was blond with very fair skin. They seemed happy and the Germans did not seem to have a problem with this, at least not that I saw. Stateside was a different story. A number of couples we knew fought hard to preserve their marriages. Marriage is hard enough under the best of circumstances, let alone being plagued with racism. Many did not survive and I cannot help but think it was due to the unnecessary stress placed on them by society. Their children also had identity problems, and why not? In a society that cannot recognize all human beings as equal, how would interracial children survive? This is yet another symptom of racism that many fight daily.

I came to realize very quickly that labels were no different then than they are today. We just work harder to be politically correct. Well, what about politically correct? I find this most interesting. In many arenas, people still tend to stereotype various groups of ethnic people into groups of acceptable terms. Many times these are regulated by the pioneers of the month rallying on the political scene. We still seem to have a problem with just calling them people. There are times I find that using descriptive terms is helpful. I find this most useful when describing someone we met somewhere and wanting a friend to meet up with them when we are not there to make proper introductions. This has become useful in my community service groups. It makes it easier to say a beautiful black woman versus the woman with the pretty face. It tends to narrow the options somewhat.

I remember addressing this issue in graduate school. I was met with resistance from a very close classmate. She seemed to say that I should find another feature to describe her. For instance, the woman with the big earrings. I had a problem with this. What if she was not wearing those earrings, and what was wrong with one's ethnic background being acknowledged? My classmate was a beautiful, strong, Puerto Rican/American Indian woman who had spent much of her life making people aware of her biases. Out of respect to her, I dropped it and realized later, when I had a chance to speak with her outside the classroom, that she was struggling with her own identity. She made the decision years ago to acknowledge her ethnicity proudly. She further educated me on how many people she knew of her background who would promote themselves as Italian in an effort to escape the typical discrimination.

It was not until graduate school, while working on my Masters in a School of Human Service, that I began to hear, listen, and experience first-hand the racism many felt throughout their lives. I had seen some of this in my undergraduate studies, but it was much more silent. Perhaps it was more open to discussion because the school had a large percentage of diverse backgrounds. I was also employed as the marketing strategist and admissions coordinator for the school. This position forced me to educate myself in the various cultural populations that the school would draw from. In the field of Human Service, it is no secret that there are many people of color and they are very well respected for their expertise. It seems to have a bit of a different twist in corporate America. There, many times due to quotas and the laws, corporations are forced to include a diverse work force. This is not to say all companies are accepting racism. Many have risen above the typical racist stereotype and have acknowledged diversity as a forum of strength.

Many times working on the road I found myself stereotyped by people of color. They assumed I felt I was above them. As I entered various agencies to conduct information sessions, I was the only white person in the room. I had no discomfort; being raised color-blind strongly came into play. Because of my comfort and acceptance of all cultures, I was quickly able to place them at ease and shared honestly, without feelings of difference. I befriended a number of people of color throughout this position and hold their friendships dear.

I must say that what we tend to speak of most are our differences. When I say differences, I mean in food, customs, dress, and how we celebrate special occasions. I have also found their views on a number of topics slightly different from the typical American. For instance, caring for grandchildren in a family of color is almost expected if needed, as opposed to some views of today. I must say this particular view is changing quickly with the increase of parents unable to care for their children, regardless of color.

I find myself reflecting back on the song by Barbara Streisand, which states that there are "no mistakes in life, just lessons learned." We can all enhance our beliefs by realizing that when we know better, we do better. However, it seems that this last statement can use some additional work. I find although people know better that they resort to their old racist views. I wonder if this is just a character flaw or a conscious decision to fight change. Change is inevitable. It is one of the few things that remains constant. We all have the choice to exploit or explore.

We have seen the merits of many people of color both professionally and personally, in sports and in upper management. These achievements have come through many struggles. They are no different than the discrimination women have endured over the years, if in nothing else to break the glass ceiling. Advancement comes slow, but it does come. Knowledge is power, and how we decide to create awareness in each of our lives will determine the thinking patterns that are seen in actions. If we are to change our belief systems or cognitive behaviors, only then can we learn from the past and view much of racism as poor behavior. In a world advertising instant gratification, it becomes difficult to work on much of anything these days. We cannot become consumed with only our own needs; we need to recycle old stuff and moved toward a more rational and humane behavior, in an effort to end racism.

Kenneth Cole had a saying on one of his shoe ads that read, "You can change an outfit, you can outfit change, or both." I found this comment most appropriate in the fight against racism. Maybe we need to hang up our old outfit of prejudice and discrimination and carefully select attire that cannot touch our lives only but those around us as well. Children are so impressionable, and as parents, we must take our role very seriously when addressing racism. After all, children model what they see and hear at home. It is important to note that as parents our awareness must be heightened to not only speak in a non-racist manner, but to act accordingly. Children are like sponges absorbing all they hear and see. As our awareness becomes more apparent, so should our choice of words and actions with our children when they witness racist behavior. If we wait for society to make the change, who knows what will happen. We certainly cannot depend on TV to give an accurate depiction of stamping out racism.

The news many times can be our greatest enemy in our fight against racism. There have been times throughout my life, in watching the news, I thought only people of color committed crimes. After all, that is what was sensationalized. As I matured, I realized the percentage is quite small compared to the white population.

As a society, what are we doing about the staggering numbers of women being left with children to care for when their husbands serve time? I have heard it is the government's problem. It is a universal problem. Regardless of race, each person is a human being and depending on their start in life, some may need help to overcome life's major obstacles. Do we help this by condemning them, or do we look within ourselves to see what changes we can instill, if only in our own communities?

Eleanor Roosevelt said, "We must preserve our right to think and differ." These differences were not meant to be used to categorize people of color. Yes, we all have differences, why not embrace them and learn, as opposed to watching and looking for flaws in these differences. Another quote I think most appropriate to this subject was by Alice Rossi: "Liberation is equally important in areas other than politics; economics, reproduction, household, sexual, and cultural emancipation are relevant." We need to look at the relevance that liberation can provide in racism.

As I revisit various thought patterns which I call "racist," I see a pattern of doing the same thing all the time. These people are getting something out of it, otherwise they would not be doing it. How do we begin to change this? We all know we cannot change anyone, only ourselves. I have come to realize that when I have made a conscious effort to change certain behavior, the side effect a number of times has been that those around me have been forced to change in some way. After all, if I stop a certain behavior, they have nowhere to attack; they stop or chose to go out and find another victim. I make this comment to impress upon people that though we cannot change others, our behavior could make small changes that may result in a positive rolling stone. Who knows where it could end up?

As I write this chapter, I feel something propelling me to work even harder at stamping out racism. We all have various gifts. I have been blessed with strong marketing and speaking skills. I will have to create an even stronger awareness within myself in an effort to educate others through my gifts. The spirit that dwells in our souls can move mountains once ignited–a force not to consider lightly.

As we became adults and became vital workers in our communities, somewhere our strong moral values have disseminated into "that religion." Religion provides a springboard in which to worship and reexamine our thoughts and actions. This is a good thing. When was the last time in our busy schedules we took the time to revisit this springboard? With the drama and hardships in our lives, I feel many of us tend to forget we have a lifeline from which to draw upon in our deepest hours. Perhaps when our faith or spirituality dwindles, the devil has a very active playing field. Now do not get me wrong, I do not want to preach to anyone, but just maybe we need to give it a fleeting thought occasionally. If you believe in the Bible, I think you will agree there was no racism within the preaching of Jesus himself. I mention this in an effort to reexamine our role models.

We need to take responsibility for the quality of our vision. This vision can take on any shape. In our many choices, we have the power to create ourselves and the voice with which we combat racism. Make no mistake, it has been, presently is, and will continue to be a constant battle. Nevertheless, like with most things in life anything worth having is worth fighting for–and in this case, fighting against. Oppression can be seen in our imagination. When we fail to imagine the humanity in other human beings we cease to grow in positive directions. We need to take the time to form an awareness that will create a formula for those who come after us to see and respect one another for their own potential.

In closing, I would like to quote Elizabeth Kulber-Ross:

> You will not grow if you sit in a beautiful flower garden, but you will grow if you are sick, if you are in pain, if you experience losses, and if you do not put your head in the sand, but take the pain and learn to accept it, not as a curse or punishment but as a gift to you with a very, very specific purpose.

We all have the ability to create a purpose in an effort to end racism. Why not put these pains to a positive, proactive approach? I ask you to reflect on the following question: What will be my approach?

CHAPTER 9
FOOL FOR THE OTHER

Bethe Hagens
The Union Institute
Cincinnati, Ohio

I've always been passionately interested in the ways people act upon that which is sacred to them. The sacred can be so blindingly simple, so deeply believed, that it may never even enter into one's conscious awareness. All my life, interracial and intercultural encounters have been sacred to me. My father introduced me to the music of Count Basie and Erroll Garner, and my mother told stories of the Indians who made camp on her family's land in Montana. Multi-racial projects in community development, the arts, education, and environmental planning make up the bulk of my resume. I have always thought that, as a professional, I could see my sacred self, my racism. As I began to write this chapter, however, I realized, somewhat painfully, that I had not seen it. Its essence has been an insidious and unbelievably powerful mythology: romantic love.

I've lived many versions of this myth and have assumed many different roles, but each has been driven by the same archetypal force–the trickster. Trickster is the shadow self, the participant observer, the fool, the outsider, the traveler. My pattern has been falling in love with "the other." This is the way I've crossed boundaries. It's been my mistaken belief that love–romantic love–is the great leveling mechanism that brings everything to a mutually understood playing field.

I'm a 60s L.A. girl, and so it's not so strange that I would believe this. I was born in Hollywood, and my parents' friends were actors. Everyone fell in love with different people, all the time. My parents were not from California, however, and so in this town where everybody was "somebody," I learned what I *was*–"a quarter Irish and English, a quarter French, half German, and a little Scotch." My high cheekbones and very dark skin suggest other genes, but "everybody" in California in the *50s* was some shade of natural or Coppertoned brown. The Hagenses, I was told, were once Huns. This explained the heavily lidded eyes I share with my father. I will never forget being asked as a teenager if I were Hopi. That was the first time I fell in love with the idea of the other.

I say all of this by way of my career as an anthropologist and musician. Over the course of my life, I've wanted to be an explorer, an architect, a rock and roll musician, and to live in the forest, hunt with a bow, gather wild food, make baskets and pottery, and wear skins. I've been able to do many of these things, and sometimes I've felt as if I live in a series of feature films. Lately, I've begun to see myself as an artist and interdisciplinary scholar. At any rate, my "culture" is, apparently, Hollywood. Fantasy, performance, and multiple roles are my taken-for-granted way of life.

I spent much of the 70s in graduate school in anthropology at the University of Chicago, playing freelance violin whenever I could. Hyde Park was everything that L.A. of the 50s and 60s was not. It was resplendently ethnic, and I felt ecstatically transparent. For my dissertation fieldwork in the Ozarks, I played fiddle and became an Anglo-Saxon hillbilly. (I became convinced that ethnicity was a product of history and politics, not genetics. At the time, this was anathema.) Later, in the 80s, I worked with a black farming cooperative as part of an NSF Community Science Residency. While I was there, I fell in love (at a distance) with Mr. Clifford Yarborough. Forty years my senior, I thought he was the smartest and most attractive man I'd ever met. He grabbed my heart in a single sentence: "If it makes me too tired to go out dancing at night, I don't do it." This was my first major awakening to personal power.

In the early 90s, I took a step back from my career. I realized that I had done just about everything I wanted to, but I was unhappy and was unsure why. Maybe it was "just" a midlife crisis, but I wanted to believe there was more involved. I took a one year leave, and ultimately resigned from, my university position to work part-time at the Union Institute (where I met Rose Duhon-Sells). I read about chaos theory, synchronicity, mythology and dreams, and intuitive knowing. I unexpectedly found my heart ensnared in an e-mail relationship in the days before they hit the tabloids. It was in that experience, which remained totally in cyberspace, and all its intensity, that I articulated my real dream.

E-mail can evoke a disarming innocence. I am one of those people who have always known that my brains are in my hands, not my head. When I sit at a keyboard, I do not know what I will write until it begins to flow from my fingers. The same thing happens when I play my violin. I create at a pace, and with an intensity, that reflects my heart. My cyber friend *appeared* to understand exactly my intentions, inflections, and nuances. We were Eros and Psyche, blind to each other but lovers nonetheless. Within that contained world, with its fixed symbols and total disregard for history or current context, we could sincerely nurture each other's souls. I will never do it again, but I will say that I know now about trance and pure intuition. I have never been in such close touch with my sacred self. From that psychic space I wrote that, if I could, I would live by the sea, in a forest, by myself, as a madwoman. I had no idea of the power of the word, or of having my words witnessed.

I began to speak my dream, to tell my story. Within less than four months, through the Internet, a Penobscot woman contacted me about renting her house on the coast of Maine. I made a visit and immediately felt as if some psychogenetic trigger had opened my awareness to another time. Everything, from the layout of her house to the smells of the coastal forest, was as I had imagined.

I still don't understand what happened. Maine, this Indian woman, and her house on the seacoast were totally familiar and totally strange. Never once had I thought about living in Maine, and yet the screenplay of my destiny seemed to be rolling just ahead of my awareness. We discovered that eight years earlier, on a one-hour excursion from Massachusetts into Maine, I had met her grandfather and bought a pair of his moccasins. On the same trip, I picked up a small beach rock that I've carried ever since. It fits my hand exactly and makes me feel safe.

The woman's brother, Dan, came by the house to meet me and to show me a Penobscot history book. It described the mythology of *baohigans,* a traditional forest creature who did the medicine man's bidding among the animal spirits. In Irish Gaelic, my name, *Bethe,* is *Bao.* And so, with no particular fanfare, Bethe Hagens was introduced to the extended family as *baohigans.* I was incredibly intrigued, yet it all seemed too much like an urban shaman woman novel. My hesitation in moving to Maine was that I knew no one but this family of Indians. At the same time, I had the absolute sense that if I did not do it, my spirit would die and I would never again follow a dream.

It's embarrassing to me now to realize how I thought about Maine: rocks, pine trees, furs, and Indians. I brought extra reams of computer paper from Chicago, a case of my favorite salad dressing, WD40, and a sheepskin coat. I bought a copier and extra violin strings. And as I was pulling away from the Chicago U-haul dealer with my former life loaded up in a truck, my car in tow behind it, the service man came running out and yelled, "Lady, lady! Remember. You can't back up!" I took it as a sign. Madwoman kicked in.

Two months after I arrived in Maine, I fell completely in love with Dan. He told me about how the stars must once have been closer to earth, about resuscitating a chipmunk with a drinking straw, about capturing a menagerie of wild mice in his cabin. When the squeaking of their treadmill began to keep him awake at night, he released them into the forest to find their way back again. I watched him play with children in the community, especially preadolescent boys whose parents worked and who simply needed consistent attention from a male. They accompanied him every-where, and the parents were totally comfortable with the situation. I watched people virtually lure him to their homes with food. Everyone said that Dan should really start a school. Dan said only that he wanted to play baseball, and he needed a team.

The kids, boys and girls alike, helped him make his Indian crafts. I remember a presentation he made at the local elementary school. He knew many of the kids, and he arrived dressed in his baseball coach uniform. As the presentation proceeded, he gradually switched costumes and became a Penobscot. I watched the children's faces change, especially when they had their time for questions. "Do you have a bathtub?" They could not believe he bought his food at Shop and Save.

Dan and I picked berries, played music, and built stuff from materials scavenged from the seacoast. One day he called a seal from a nearby island to shore. Another day he arrived all excited that we might be able to make ice hockey goals from a heavy nylon fishing net that had washed up on shore and was caught under the dock. Our lives meshed this way. My position in a cyber university is very freely structured, and Dan's job is life. Family and friends provide the context in which he can live this way. I watched him borrow my car for days on end and drink all the Diet Pepsi I could keep in the refrigerator. I believed he was the medicine man, Buddha in a baseball cap. I still do.

Like his grandfather, Chief To-Me-Kin, Dan is a man of carefully chosen words. Very early on in our friendship, he told me that I was too serious. Yes, we might be dreaming exactly the same dreams. Yes, I might be *Baohigans.* But no, he was not in love with me. For years, I didn't believe him. His behaviors toward me were those I'd come to recognize as distinct signs of courtship. He'd introduced me to all of his friends and we spent lots of time together. I cooked for him, we shared money, and he brought his friends by. The kids he knew used my house and phone as their contact for Dan.

Dan's mother began to invite me to all the family celebrations. His sister told the people at church that the angels had brought me to them. It was overwhelming and confusing to me. As I became more intertwined with dozens of other family members, I could see that Dan did not feel like a brother or "just a friend." He also did not feel like a lover. If the script was not to fall in love, marry, and wear skins, what was it? This went on for five years. I began to wonder why I was even "with" these people, because they were Indians? There it was: racism.

In fact, though, I really loved the entire bunch. I wanted context and family so badly, in the peculiarly Indian way in which it was being offered to me, that I decided to "love" Dan unconditionally, whatever that might mean. At times it was agony, letting go of the romantic love, because there was no "talking about it." What needed to be said had been said, and I found that the images in my dreams told me absolutely everything I needed to know anyway. Oddly enough, the culture of fantasy I knew as a child of Hollywood was not unlike the day-to-day mythic consciousness of the Penobscots. I had become a madwoman, *baohigaizs,* and in the process had gained conscious access to my own sacred self

My inner work became clear. I needed to detoxify looking at my myth of romance. I went through my journal and found dozens of notations about Dan and his family, me and Dan, Dan and community, Dan and me and community. One part of me actively imagined that we would be married and live happily ever after in a tepee in his grandmother's yard. Another part thought we would build a replica Penobscot lodge as a performing arts and sports center with a million dollar grant Dan would get from the National Endowment and some (as yet unnamed) Native American foundation.

The lodge and the marriage never happened, but we did end up forming a rock and roll band, and we practice every week in the basement at Dan's mom's house (where he lives). Dan risks more, and I am much less serious. Most of all, Dan needs total freedom to wander. Apparently, so do I. Gradually, my "work" has become my life and "career" now seems an incredibly foreign concept. I need the extended family and community rituals associated with baseball, games at the beach, and playing ice hockey on the neighborhood pond. The policy culture I lived in prior to moving to Maine would label some of our behavior as codependent and dysfunctional. I don't see it that way anymore. I see our friendship in the context of what I imagine close-knit Indian life in Maine must once have been.

I continue to be absolutely amazed by the amount of time this family spends just being in each other's presence, telling stories, and offering unconditional support. They live in what I know as "Beauty Way," though they don't use this terminology. Their lives are far from ideal, and they have as many problems as anyone else. Still, the genuine compassion and humor of these people is absolutely true to what I know (as an anthropologist) about Penobscots. Life here is not at all what I had expected, and it is unlike anything I've experienced previously. I can't describe it. I recognize it, know it intuitively, but I know I don't quite understand it. My mouth tastes different when I enter Gramma Ranco's house, but this has nothing to do with smell. It comes up from the heart. I feel a genuine Bethe emerge. I feel Indian, but not as a role, or genetics, or an image. I think this is where the real elimination of racism in society may begin.

CHAPTER 10
THE DEVIL CAN'T TAKE MY JOY: LIVING IN SPITE OF RACISM

Cynthia L. Jackson
The Union Institute
Cincinnati, Ohio

The rise of the black American from slavery to citizenship is one of the most dramatic chapters of American history. It is a continuing process, the pace of which has been a source of national disgrace. Nevertheless, to the heirs of the slaves, there has been left a legacy of black experiences–with its triumphs, pain, and joy–that constitutes a unique record of the indomitability of the human spirit. The black experience expresses the hopes of the past, present, and future, soaked with the blood, sweat, and tears of black Americans interwoven into the fiber of a country that negates their humanity. In the United States, everyday blacks have to deal with the issue of race and racism. Racism dominates the collective psyches of black Americans. It is plausible, even in the threshold of the 21st century, that whites can live their entire life, if they so choose, denying the existence of racism and their role in perpetuating it.

Many whites have never, and will never be, willing to acknowledge the gulf of culture, history, and reality between themselves and blacks, and the legitimacy of these differences. Too many whites continue to present their experiences as representing THE American experience. Everyday in the United States, Americans are consumed with job pressures, health, and family concerns, to name a few. These issues alone create their own, often overwhelming, challenges for living. Now couple these challenges with the intense social and emotional experience that is characteristic of racism and one only has a sense of the weight of oppression that is carried everyday by blacks and others of color, regardless of class, education, and gender.

Blacks achieve a sense of their own identity from their own experiences. Being black is a state of mind reflecting the unique experiences shared by blacks, varied, as they are, that set them apart from any other group and results in a certain kind of psychological adjustment that other groups do not have to make. Blacks have to develop a kind of mental toughness and survival skills, in terms of coping with life, that has enabled them to exist in an environment that is sometimes both complicated and hostile, but almost always hostile (Jackson, 1970).

This chapter will look at institutional racism in the United States and living a full life, not surviving, in spite of racism. The position I take in this chapter is based on history and my experiences. In this chapter, white is used as a convenient nomenclature for saying institutional racism. The terms "black" and "African American" are not used interchangeably. Blacks galvanize all people of the African Diaspora. African American refers to blacks who are citizens of the United States. The views and examples shared are expressed through my lens as a black person. However, the reader should be aware that similar experiences occur for all people of color in the United States. The lenses through which the experiences are viewed and analyzed are different because of each group's history in the United States.

The Power of Racism

Racism is about power. It is the power of one group in a society to exclude, marginalize, and practice a subscribed doctrine of nihilism against another group or groups. Racism remains the most powerful institution in the United States. Racism is a human rights issue. Few whites in the United States perceive that there is a greater comfort to look outward for the denial of human rights than to look inward. Nihilism and genocide can be physical, psychological, and emotional.

Racism is based on the predetermined reasoning that whites are superior to all other races, simply because they are white. To reinforce this absurd notion, is the mythology of American history. Racism can either be individual or institutional. Both are harmful and can be destructive to the recipients. Individual racism is a one–on–one situation. It is usually quite blatant and can be seen for what it is. This type of racism can be addressed head on, and while not alleviating or eliminating racism it is one that is manageable.

Most whites will openly condemn individual acts of racism. But whites tend not to think about racism unless it is thrown in their face. This should not be surprising. How often do people voluntarily think of a societal issue, worry about it, and become consumed about its injustice and repercussions when they do not believe it is influencing them in the first place?

The more detrimental and subtle form of racism is institutional racism. Institutional racism is inherent in the policies, practices, and institutional missions that have been established and respected by whites in United States society. This is primarily because these behaviors support whites' status in this society.

More than a hundred years have passed since legal slavery was abolished. Yet, blacks are not liberated. We have made, and will continue to make, contributions in the arts, sciences, industry, technology, the humanities, and other fields of endeavor too numerous to name. Simultaneously, we struggle to establish identity with our heritage, to write the story of our roles and contributions to the great achievements of the United States (Jackson, 1970).

Willie Lynch School of Black Subservience

In 1712, a British slave owner from the West Indies was invited to speak to slave owners in the Virginia colony. The purpose of the speech was to explain how to implement his "program" for black subservience. He also wrote a letter to colonial United States slave owners titled, "Let's Make a Slave." The conceiver of the "program" for black subservience was William Lynch, a.k.a. Willie Lynch. (Spann, 1970). Willie Lynch was probably the single most influential person to institutionalize slavery in the United States. In his letter and speech he described his success in controlling blacks.

He begins with his "Cardinal Principles for Making a Negro."

1. Both horse and niggers are no good to the economy in the wild or natural state.
2. Both must be broken and tied together for orderly production.
3. For orderly future, special and particular attention must be paid to the female and the youngest offspring.
4. Both must be crossbred to produce a variety and division of labor.
5. Both must be taught to respond to a peculiar new language.
6. Psychological and physical instruction of containment must be created for both. (Lynch, 1712)

Embracing these principles, Lynch explains that these principles are "for long-range comprehensive economic planning. For fear that future generations may not understand the principle of breaking both horse and men, we lay down the art" (Lynch, 1712).

To implement his principles, the "art" was based on creating an environment of distrust by focusing on differences. Thus, light-skinned blacks are pitted against dark-skinned blacks, the "house" black against the "field" black, females against males, educated blacks against less educated blacks, younger blacks against older blacks, and the list goes on. He guaranteed that if installed correctly, it would control the slaves for at least 300 years. This indoctrination, shall carry on and will become self-refusing and self-generating for hundreds maybe thousands of years (Lynch, 1712).

In program development it is generally agreed that program adoption occurs through seven levels of use that describe *behaviors* of the users: non-use, orientation, preparation, mechanical use, routine, refinement, integration, renewal (Hall et. al., 1975). It is safe to say that Willie Lynch was probably one of the most successful program developers in history.

Today, Willie Lynch's "program" functions at the renewal level of use. The renewal level is defined as:

> . . . the user [reevaluating] the quality of use of the innovation, seeks major modifications of or alternative to present innovation to achieve increased impact on clients, examines new developments in the field, and explores new goals for self and the system. (p. 54)

Willie Lynch's "program" clearly explains the principles of racism. More importantly, it can serve as a blueprint to develop models to break the psychological, emotional and economic slavery cycle that continues to exist for blacks.

African Americans were given a false sense of security of their status in the post-Civil Rights era. Those who bought into this security measured their success on how much they could distance themselves from other blacks, and on how much their lives and accomplishments resembled those of whites. The current influence of Willie Lynch is demonstrated in the rift between blacks who are for Affirmative Action and those who are against it. It would be laughable, if it was not so sad, to hear them talk about being self-made, pulling themselves up by their own boot straps, achieving with no help from other blacks. Whether or not they want to admit it, Affirmative Action got them where they are.

African American baby boomers got their toes in the door of many sectors in the United States because of Affirmative Action. Whether they got in the door through organizational conscious or quotas, it boils down to black access in education, employment, and life styles in the past 40 years is in large part due to Affirmative Action.

Acceptance

Blacks, although freed by law, continue to be enslaved by practices against which laws offer no protection. Basic citizenship rights that should have made it possible for blacks to share equally in the benefits and achievements of the "American Dream," became the rights we had to fight for rather than them being our birthrights. It seems the fight is never over. We have to be vigilant, continually and consistently. The Civil Rights acts are a clear example of this. Civil Rights legislation grants blacks the right to have certain citizenship privileges that whites take for granted. Thus the legal concept of "protected class."

The first Civil Rights acts were in the 1860s. These were short lived and only tacitly enforced. By the time the Civil Rights acts of the 1960s were passed into law, one would have never known that these acts were not new, but rather a reenactment of 100 years earlier. Now at the threshold of the 21st century, once again we (all U.S. citizens) could find ourselves in the same situation.

We are past the legislation stage of alleviating racism. Laws alone are not going to address the issue of institutional racism. Civil Rights laws, which once kept pace for equity, are being dismantled, such as Affirmative Action, or will soon expire, such as the Voter Rights Act.

We are at the heart–and–mind stage of alleviating racism, a stage that requires individuals to take a look at themselves and decide what is right, fair and just. Being politically correct is not enough.

Civil rights legislation is based on the underlying principle of tolerance–whites tolerating people of color. As tolerant people, whites can be viewed as the victims–long-suffering, giving tacit permission, and being resigned to the fact that blacks are not going anywhere. Desegregation is tolerance. Tolerance may have been appropriate in the 1950s and 1960s, where civil rights for all in America was once again a novel concept, but it is unacceptable in the 21st century.

Obviously civil rights legislation is not enough either. While enforcement is necessary, that enforcement must be accompanied with the sentiment of the American public that civil rights for all are both necessary and legitimate.

Integration did not work and is inappropriate. Integration, like assimilation, requires one group to totally lose its cultural identity, and become like another group. Racism can only be alleviated when white Americans operate at a level of acceptance. Acceptance of individuals, cultures, languages, thoughts, histories, contributions, ways of life, and real concern on addressing the issues in America such as illiteracy, health, economics, employment, and housing without prejudice. However, acceptance is a higher plane than tolerance. Acceptance requires welcoming, encountering, and respecting.

The United States is not close to living in racial acceptance. Practices and attitudes have created stereotypes and myths about the character of blacks that whites still readily accept. Two examples come to mind. First, there is a rise of white supremacy groups. The need for hate crime legislation speaks volumes on the status of race relations in the United States.

Second, in this racist society, a Susan Smith can still have whites believe that a black man kidnapped her children. The irony of this is that the black community never believed it. Not because of naiveté, but because of reality. In a town the size of a dot, Union, South Carolina, a black man alone with two white children would draw attention. Yet, the United States was ready to believe that far-fetched story. While believing her story, over 200 black men in Georgia, South Carolina, and North Carolina were detained. Granted that after she was found to be lying, blacks received an apology. The apology was not enough. In the 1990s, the situation should not have been able to happen.

Keeping Racism Alive

Blacks are not a novelty in the United States. We have been here for over 400 years. Twenty-six blacks were on the Mayflower. Those 26 were not slaves. They arrived on these shores as indentured servants, as many whites did. Over a 25-year period, it became increasingly difficult for blacks to buy their freedom. Blacks moved from the legal status of indentured servants to permanent servants, and finally to the legal status of slaves. This established slavery in the United States as a recognized institution.

In spite of the cruel system of slavery, blacks found strength to rebel against it. These rebellions reflected the courage of blacks, working in slavery and subjection, to gain freedom for themselves by purchase, by flight, and by insurrection. Denmark Vesey and Nat Turner led two of the most well known rebellions.

Today there are two groups keeping racism alive. First, there are whites. Through their policies, practices, and institutional missions, the institution of racism is perpetuated because it serves the needs of whites and is to their advantage to do so.

Finally, there are the blacks who are too scared to take a stand. In spite of their frustration and angst, they believe that it is better to keep what they have than push the envelope. Believe it or not, there was a large number of these blacks during the Civil Rights Movement of the 1960s. They contribute to the perpetuation of racism because they allow whites to have power over them, and keep them fearful, subservient and almost grateful for any crumb that is thrown their way.

Alleviating Racism through a New Nationalism

There are two major focuses in the world going on simultaneously: new nationalism and globalism. These focuses are mutually reciprocal.

Nationalism, by definition, concentrates on the needs of a nation. Those needs are directed to be concerned with only what occurs in the boundaries of a nation. New nationalism is not constrained by the artificial boundaries of land. It concentrates on the needs of individuals based on race, religion, language, tribal traditions, and cultural identifies. Thus, when speaking of the African Diaspora, one must embrace people on every continent.

As we wrestle with the expansion of the new nationalism, and discard old paradigms to replace them with radically new ones, we find ourselves in a world that focuses on globalism, also. At first glance it may seem that new nationalism and globalism are contradictions. This is not the case. As we shift paradigms on what is a nation, we come to realize that a nation is people, not land territories and boundaries. To develop the new nations, we are forced to approach the task globally.

Two Paths to Address Racism

Given all of the forces that work diligently and deliberately to keep racism alive, it would appear at first look that the power of racism is so overwhelming that nothing can be done. One may not be able to change the world, but one can change his/her world that is in his/her span of control. There are two ways to change your world. You can choose to change it as a brute force, or you can change it as a vital force. Both ways can be effective.

As a brute force, you focus on those who perpetuate racism. You are trying to reason with whites, black parasites, and scared blacks. You confront and demand. Your focus is on the negative aspects of living in a racist society. In my younger days, I subscribed to the methods of brute force. For me, brute force sapped my energy because I was actively angry all of the time. It was a type of anger that was detrimental to me physically, emotionally, and psychologically. My anger was becoming a true hate that was consuming me.

In the past six years, I have chosen the path of being a vital force. I am like a blade of grass breaking through cement. Instead of focusing on whites, black parasites, and scared blacks to address racism, I focus on blacks who are ready for a change. I work with them to strengthen our forces to increase our cooperation and collaboration in becoming self-sufficient. I do this by providing opportunities through access to education. Self-sufficient does not mean separate. Rather it is the ability to contribute to the common good of the United States and the world on our terms. To be self-sufficient is true liberation. The new nationalism is about being self-sufficient. I do not limit myself to blacks who live in the United States. There is strength in numbers. Our numbers are many and the possibilities are greater when the focus is on the African Diaspora.

In its collaborative and cooperative context, education can provide a means to the economic and social development of people. Education can empower individuals to contribute to the development process of their own lives and those of others. Willie Lynch taught blacks to focus on our differences, whereby collaboration and cooperation cannot occur. I am a proponent of focusing on our similarities.

I firmly believe that for the people of the African Diaspora, education and research is what will build the infrastructure to globally combat racism and develop a new nationalism. My work at the Union Institute with the HBCU initiative, Caribbean Network of Scholars, and the African Doctoral Program are examples of my being a vital force for the new nationalism.

Closing

The present and future will continue to hold many struggles for blacks and their allies in identifying and removing the structural and attitudinal blocks preventing black America from achieving liberation and full and equal participation in every phase of life in this country and the world. We have, we are, and we shall continue to press determinedly and successfully toward the goal of ultimate liberation and of equality before the law and, more importantly, equality of opportunity for all.

References

Hall, G.E., et al. (1975). *Levels of use of the innovation: A framework for analyzing innovative adoption.* **Journal of Teacher Education,** *26,* 52-56.

Jackson, W.S. (1970). **Thoughts on the black experience.** Unpublished manuscript.

Lynch, W. (1712). **Let's make a slave.** (Speech and letter.) http//:www.carlnelson.com.

Spann, K.T. (Compiler & Editor). (1970). **Willie Lynch's 'let's make a slave.** (Available from Black Arcade Liberation Library.)

CHAPTER 11
RACE RELATION ORIENTATION
OF MY CHILDHOOD

Angela C. May
The Union Institute
Cincinnati, Ohio

In many ways, my experiences with race relations during my formative years were very unusual for an African American girl growing up in inner-city Detroit. My family, which consisted of my older sister and brother, my mother, maternal great-aunt, and maternal great-grandmother (my father visited on the weekends and occasionally during the weekdays, as my parents were separated), lived in a large house on an historical, residential boulevard. My maternal great-grandmother purchased the house, which is still in my family today, in the early 1950s. Although there was a heavy Jewish population at that time, it slowly evolved into what is now considered one of Metro-Detroit areas for old black money and for new upwardly mobile black families as well.

As I attempt to recall adult conversations during those formative years. I am hard-pressed to remember the few statements that were made about our being black. I do, however, remember my grandmother's concern for, "the black man," and what would become of him. She knew then, as did her mother before her, that a plague was on the horizon and would likely render many of our people an endangered species. Although my great-grandmother died the year before I was born, I was told that she spoke of the drugs that would consume so many of the black Americans. This of course, was decades before anyone was concerned about a drug epidemic.

My orientation in terms of race relations was unusual, in my mind, because I was never raised to think of myself as being a color first. My being black was simply one of the many aspects of my person, but far from a defining image of myself. We were raised to consider first that we were children of God, then part of the May family which meant that we must carry ourselves with pride, dignity, and respect. The idea that I could be anything and anyone that I chose to be was simply part of every-day life, and no one thought otherwise.

I was most fortunate in the fact that I was exposed to people of a variety of backgrounds very early in life. From Kindergarten to mid-way through the fourth grade, I attended one of the Detroit Public Schools. I then transferred, along with my older brother, to Peace Lutheran. This was a small Lutheran school in Utica, Michigan, a semi-rural suburb many miles outside of the city, where I spent the second half of the 4th grade through the 12th grade. My brother and I were the only two people of color in the entire school. This was an interesting experience. Up to that point, my brother and I were always considered to be very light-skinned people because our complexions are a very light brown; what many folks referred to as "high yellow" complexioned African Americans. Now, suddenly, we were in a world where we were the darkest people in the building, even if the difference was only by a shade. For me, it was a fascinating experience to feel myself change from "light-bright" to very dark in a matter of minutes, simply because of a change in environment.

This taught me first-hand the valuable lesson that only I can decide who and what I am. They said that I was dark. Dark compared to what? At home, I am light. Can it be that I really change colors just because I cross the line that divides the city and the suburbs? No. I remain the same in reality, but I could feel myself changing, as the eyes of others began to perceive me as "different." The host of ignorance that accompanied their assumption of who and what we were fascinated and irritated my brother and me. We visited their homes and met their families. Most of them were nice, Lutheran, God-fearing people who were making a living but were hardly well-off financially. Yet their lack of education regarding the reality of life in the Big City had them believing that we dodged bullets constantly, that we lived in abject poverty, and so forth. My mother, brother, and I took it upon ourselves to educate them to the facts of the matter. While many of them typically lived in simple, one- or two-story homes that were built a decade or so prior to their purchase, we lived on a beautiful tree-lined historical boulevard in which black doctors, lawyers, and Indian Chiefs were one's neighbors. They were shocked to discover that these blacks from Detroit lived in a 17-room home built with all the ornate artistry for which the homes of 1917 were known. With five bedrooms, five bathrooms, two back porches, and a third floor apartment that was designed for the maid's quarters, this was not the house of abject poverty.

This experience was my first lesson in understanding that there is a whole set of assumptions that accompany the idea that one is black in America. As the American mentality dictates, those assumptions must necessarily include being ignorant, uneducated, and poverty stricken. While I knew that in reality I did not change shape or color simply because I stepped into their presence, I could actually feel my image change before my very eyes. I knew what I symbolized for them each time that they looked at me. While this prejudiced mentality did begin to change over time as my family educated our classmates and teachers alike, this helped to shape in my own mind what being black in America really means. It also demonstrated to me how lack of exposure could truly limit the understanding of others and affect one's perspective. In terms of my own perspective, I am ever glad that, unlike many of my fellow folks of color, I was never under the impression that being Caucasian meant being well-off or rich in any way. I certainly never felt that they were in any way better than myself, merely because of their skin color. The two ideas were simply not synonymous in my mind, basically because I saw for myself that I, my family, and other blacks in my life were often better off financially, culturally, and spiritually than most of the white people in my life. While these were some of my first lessons regarding race relations, they would not be the last.

As my sister before me, I attended the Academy of the Sacred Heart, an all girls high school in Bloomfield Hills, Michigan, about 30 minutes outside of Detroit. Now this was a complete 360-degree turn from my Peace Lutheran days. Bloomfield Hills is located in one of the wealthiest suburbs in the country. Let us simply say that I spent my high school days with girls whose families made their money in oil–and I do not mean working at the local Shell gas station. These were the families who *owned* the local Shell gas station, and the wells that produced that petroleum as well. While my education at A.S.H. was extremely valuable to me (I drew upon it even through to my doctorate program), some of its most valuable aspects was again the opportunity to experience the people. I never really had any preconceived notions about "rich people" as being anything different or special. This was primarily because we were raised to see each person through God's eyes. Their material possessions were of no consequence and were not something by which to be impressed. Attending Sacred Heart was for me the chance to solidify these ideas, because truly the daughters of millionaires were no different than those of factory workers. I saw young ladies who struggled with self-esteem issues, alcoholism, neglectful parents, and so forth, and felt compassion for many of them. These issues seemed not to be isolated to any one race, but I could see them surface with girls from varying backgrounds. While most of the girls at A.S.H. were Caucasian, several were of Indian parentage (from India), some were African American, and a few were of Asian decent. Many of the painful, life-changing issues that they had to face did not seem to vary based upon the color of their skin.

This experience helped to further shape my understanding that being black in America has to do with a culture that is defined more by the perspectives of the society in which we have developed, and less by our monetary gain or lack thereof. I saw for myself that a person of color may actually have money and position, but is still considered a second class citizen based solely on the color of their skin.

Life Experiences that Shaped My Current Attitude About Racism

Allow me first to state my current attitudes about racism. My beliefs about racism are much the same as my beliefs about sexism. I tend to believe that women and men have much more in common with each other than they have that differs from one another. My experiences in life, as well as my experiences as a psychologist, have reinforced this idea over time. Women and men want and desire the same things: respect, love, strength, power, the opportunity to procreate, and so forth. The differences may lie in how we go about accomplishing these things. But even in such instances, these differences may not be nearly as exaggerated as many "experts" would have us think.

By the same token, I have learned that racism serves the same purpose as the supposed "battle of the sexes"–it is calculated to divide us. Show me you a person who practices hatred of others based upon racial or ethnic makeup, and I will show a person who indulges in self-hate. I say this because the reality is that, of the many species that walk the earth, humans are the most similar to one another. The ways in which we differ are so minute that to hate another person because of a skin difference means that one is hating someone who, for all intents and purposes, is almost exactly like us. Regardless of the racial makeup, most of us have two arms, two legs, a pair of eyes, one nose, one mouth, and so forth. When we look at another person, even if the skin color is darker or lighter, we are looking at mirror images of ourselves (e.g., one head, one brain, similar life aspirations, same needs, etc.).

Therefore, the question becomes that if all humans are primarily the same creatures, what purpose does racial hate serve, particularly since race is a nebulous concept at best? Certainly the color of one's skin is no indication of who that person is, considering that Hispanics can look as white as Ricky Ricardo or as black as the dark skinned contemporary singer John Secada. And certainly the color of one's skin tells us nothing of the individual or the background of that person. This is especially true considering the fact that African Americans are known as the "rainbow race," with not only our skin color but also our facial features, running the gamut from Southern African looking features to Northern European looking facial features and hair texture.

While on the surface racial hatred is meant to divide people from each other and to separate us in terms of mentality as well as economic well being, it can be seen as a form of self-hatred as well. People of color can represent to others a part of themselves that they wish to ignore, just as men have relegated women to third and fourth class citizens of fear of the power that women represent. The stereotype of the "happy darky dancing in the fields" is a derogatory concept, accepted by the masses for centuries. This is not just a way to alleviate the guilt that the "darkies" are out in the field in the first place, but also a way to explain away the ability to tap into that spiritual, unnamed self. This is a self who can hear and interpret the music of the ancestors, the music of the heart. For one whose traditions dictate that such experiences are pagan and foreign to "refined" persons, the idea that persons who are not of color might have the capacity to feel such spiritual awakenings can be a terrifying concept. In my travels around the world, especially to certain parts of Europe (such as Italy, England, and Ireland) and many of the Balkan states, I discovered how beloved the American Negro Spiritual is.

In every place to which we traveled, the music that was most requested was the Spiritual. Why? Our unique experiences as stolen people were not shared in necessarily the same way as the tribulations of other peoples. Yet, everywhere that we traveled, people were able to feel, and intuitively understand, the nature of the broken heart and the idea of a triumphant spirit, regardless of their background. This crystallized for me even more acutely the reality that we are all the same people, beneath the skin color. The Bible scripture that teaches us to "love thy neighbor as thyself" has a message regarding this issue that I believe too many of us miss. On the surface we are instructed to love our neighbor, that other person. But more deeply still we are taught first to love ourselves; the point being that how you treat the other person is actually predicated on how you treat yourself first. Therefore, you cannot love another unless first you love yourself, and by the same token you cannot hate another unless you first experience self-hate.

One of the experiences that most profoundly affected my current attitude about racism was my family's assumption that we were equally as valuable as any person, regardless of skin color or background. In fact, the worth of a person in my family was always based upon what that person did for Jesus. There was no other criterion. Whenever my people dealt with others, their being white or otherwise was never an issue. They were simply people that we knew.

In addition to my family background, the opportunity to travel the world during my later teens and my 20s contributed a great deal to my own perceptions of racism. I have been blessed with the opportunity to travel as a soloist with the Marygrove College Chamber Singers to Limerick, Cork, and Dublin Ireland; to Riga; Lithuania; Minsk (Detroit's sister city) Leningrad; Moscow; and Vilnius in the former USSR; and to Stratford and London England. I was also able to travel, as part of a group of students from the Union Institute in Cincinnati, Ohio, to South Africa during my days as a doctorate student. In addition, I traveled with family and friends as a tourist to Greece, Turkey, London, Paris, Florence, Rome, Venice, Barbados, Mexico, Jerusalem, Egypt, and Bethlehem. These experiences taught me much about how the world views racism, and particularly African Americans.

I discovered, as many who travel abroad have found, that people of color from America are first and foremost considered Americans. This was a huge surprise to many of the people who traveled in these parties who were used to being seen as a skin color first and foremost. Non-Americans tended, in my experience, to lump us all together in the category of "American," and it made no difference to them if the Yankee was Caucasian from Boston, or African American from the South side of Chicago.

The second lesson learned from traveling abroad was that there is an assumption out there where African Americans are concerned. First of all, there seems to be a pervasive attitude that Americans in general are "loose" individuals who party constantly, Hollywood style. Added to this is the idea that female Americans are particularly open to this kind of lifestyle. I personally found this to be quite a shocking revelation. Certainly this is not to say that every person envisioned that we were living this lifestyle, but I did find repeatedly the same attitude in many of the European and Eastern European locations. However, I was perhaps most shocked and dismayed to discover that it was the black American woman who was considered to have the least inhibitions, and the lowest moral fiber. Again, I emphasize that this by no means depicts the thoughts of every person in every European location. But the idea seemed to be accepted in several places that I visited. This saddened me because I was well aware that these images did not come out of a vacuum, but were fed by our American media. It indicated to me that, even though both Caucasian and African Americans were seen as part of the same land first and foremost, the same racist attitudes that are so pervasive in our country infect the minds of those abroad as well.

The Politics of Racism in Society

There is an aspect of race relations that I have found that is not addressed in our society nearly to the degree that the politics of skin color has been. That is the issue of class. On many occasions I have talked with people who have told me about experiences that they may have had with one entity or another, perhaps a restaurant or other place of business, in which they were treated less than appropriately. The natural inclination by many of us is to assume that racism is afoot if the establishment is white-owned and run. What I have found is that, unfortunately, this is often the case, and even in situations where racism is not really the issue, in the context of our history it makes sense to jump to this conclusion.

However, there is another aspect to this issue, and it is one of class-ism. While often times classism and racism go hand in hand, they are not always synonymous. I have observed, from my own experience, that one individual of color can be treated unfairly by an establishment, and another individual of color can be treated quite well by that same establishment. Why does this happen when they are both black? Certainly other layers of prejudicial thought come into play, such as the hue of one's skin. I am not unaware of the fact that I may get better treatment than my darker skinned brother or sister because I am lighter skinned. By the same token, I am also aware that my being female, and considered attractive, plays a part in the treatment that I receive as well. Within the context of racism, when there is the situation of two people of color, and the treatment differs, is this difference necessarily due to racism in every instance?

While classism is often inherent in racist thought and treatment (heretofore referred to as the difference between the house slave and the field slave), it is my belief that there are circumstances in which classism alone is the explanation for unfair treatment.

While we cannot always know what lies behind the prejudicial acts of others, I do believe that it behooves each one of us to take a close look at each circumstance to try and understand what is at work. Speaking from my own experiences, there have been establishments that have treated my colleagues less than fairly, but had treated my companions and myself with the utmost in courteous service. Now, this by no means indicates that I have not experienced racism in my life. This also does not indicate that, solely because I may have had a positive experience in the same places where others did not, that racism was not an issue. I am simply suggesting that in any instance where racism may be the culprit, let us investigate it and refuse to tolerate it, but let us also be aware that the "-isms" come in many forms.

There are times when one ism (e.g., sexism) attaches itself to another (e.g., racism) and it becomes more difficult to tell what it is that we are dealing with. But in an effort to keep the fight against racism strong and not let others accuse us of crying wolf one too many times, it becomes necessary not to dilute the argument by assuming racism at every juncture. In my own life, I have often jokingly stated that I never know which of the "-isms" for which I am being attacked, considering that I am a walking compilation of three: young, black and female. I have occasionally run into individuals who have had a problem with me, particularly since I became a doctor of psychology. In my opinion, it would not make sense to automatically assume that the problem lies in my being African American, considering that there may be several reasons for such a reaction. In fact, since completing the doctorate degree, it has been most instructive to me that more people have had difficulty with the concept of me as a doctor because of my age (I recently had my 32nd birthday) first, and my gender and race as secondary factors. It is important to be aware that oftentimes people are threatened by others for a variety of reasons, and hanging the banner of racism on the fact every time detracts from the issue. And it is not only the victim that does this, but the perpetrator as well. In the mentality of our country, when all else fails, we call our feelings of dislike of another person racism, simply because the object of one's distaste is of another racial background. Of course, this is often the case, but there are also times in which personality differences are the underlying reason. Furthermore, the same factors would be at work even if the individuals were of the same racial background, because the same personality is present. We are not always aware of this, however, because we are blinded by our near obsession with racist thought in this country.

Methods I have used to Addressed Racist Behavior in My Presence

Whenever I have faced racist behavior in the past, I typically address it in two ways:

1. Through education as to the reality of being black in America.
2. By drawing parallels between people of color and whites.

I always try to approach it as an opportunity to educate, as I am acutely aware that so much of the racism that is out there is the result of ignorance. I attempt to allow the other person to see that, while I have unique qualities, some of them are due to my being a black American, while many other qualities are due to other reasons. In trying to address the racist mentality, I attempt to help the other person understand vast experiences that African Americans have had, as a means of helping them to understand that our culture is as diverse as any other. Moreover, being African American does not mean being poor, uneducated, drug addicted, and violent. Instead, I paint the picture that allows them, hopefully, to see that being African American means being poor, middle class, rich, quiet, loud, educated, uneducated, drug-free, drug-addicted, and so forth. In other words, we try to explain to others that we are no more to be pigeonholed into two or three categories than any other culture.

In attempting to draw parallels between people of color and whites, I attempt to help the person see that we are far more alike than we are different. First, as human beings, we both want healthy, happy families. We both want meaningful work and to feel valued. By doing this, I try to break down the barriers that ignorance and several centuries of propaganda-like messages have helped to erect regarding how "different" and unalike whites and blacks really are. In all of this, I attempt to help them see that they are being prejudicial, even if not consciously so. I typically ask several questions about why they say what they do, or why they think a certain way. This often leads me to share experiences with them that let them know that, though we differ in skin color, we might come from a similar background. I do this in an effort to eliminate the classism that often comes with racism.

Once I have made these statements, I then typically attempt to educate them as to the truth about the black Experience in America: that in reality it has nothing to do with where you come from, but rather with how you are perceived and treated. This makes the experience real. No matter where we originate, we are perceived as less educated and less qualified than our Caucasian counterparts. While this is hardly a revelation, it is interesting to note the surprise on the faces of many whites who naturally assumed that being from the ghetto was what gave you the experience of being black. The shocked expression remains in place as they realize that it was not the limited exposure and substandard education that was the explanation for why you did not get that job for which you applied. Many people who are not of color have been truly amazed when they recognize that you, too, may have attended the Academy of the Sacred Heart, but were discriminated against nonetheless because your skin was not light enough.

Elements that My Observations May
Contribute to the Alleviation of Racism in Society

Perception of Self

I often tell people that the best way to choose a living is to do what you are. For example, I am a psychologist because I love to help people and I am intrigued by the reasons that they behave as they do. If I did not get paid for what I do, I would continue to observe people because it is part of who I am. This is also true for my career as a professional vocalist. If no one came to listen to the sound of my voice ever again, I would continue to sing because it is what I love to do.

By the same token, it has been my observation that racism, or any hatred-based thought process, for that matter, gets its first life's breath from one's sense of self. Simply put, the way that one sees oneself will tell you much about how that person will perceive and treat others. It is for this reason that in a standard psychological evaluation, for example, psychologists always inquire as to the quality of relationships in the person's life. Of course, there are many reasons for the mining of this useful information. However, one of the chief reasons that we ask these questions is because the nature of one's interactions with others in the world can speak volumes about how that person values himself or herself.

Self-Esteem

I have noted that the more secure a person becomes with herself or himself, the less likely the need to put others down in any way. My grandmother used to say that parents have to teach children how to love. In other words, children must be shown what respect for others looks like. They need to be taught, in words and (oftentimes most importantly) in deeds, how consideration and compassion for others manifests itself. To borrow from the famous theorist Maslow, who developed the hierarchy of needs theory, a person must first satisfy the need for survival and a strong sense of self-worth before he or she is able to give to others. Speaking hypothetically, if this is the case, then by the same token if a person does not have a strong sense of self-worth and thus lowered self-esteem, then he or she would be more likely to feel the need to take from others rather than to give to them. The idea of taking from others can manifest itself in many forms, such as making derogatory statements, minimizing them as less valuable, and scapegoating. It has been my observation that the most insecure individuals who possess a need to place others beneath them in some way, (due to a lack of or weakened sense of self-worth) are the people who tend to be racist.

Racism = Hatred

I have therefore come to the conclusion that truly loving people cannot be racist. Why? The reason is because racism and love are complete opposites and cannot occupy the same space at the same time. Loving people means that you want to believe the best about them. It means that you want to invest in the idea that they can be as good or better than you. Racism subscribes to the concepts of selfishness, not love (e.g., "*You* cannot be as good as me. Only I am superior, you must be beneath me"). This is not to suggest that a person cannot vacillate between beliefs from one moment to the next. But, in that second in which racial hatred is accepted and/or acted upon, that is the moment in which the individual is a hateful person. Either you are a hateful person who practices this habit of thought in one form or another, or you are a loving person who practices loving kinds of behavior and thought in its many forms. Webster defined racism in terms of the belief in superiority or dominance of one person over another based upon race. Definitions of love, however, involve a different kind of mentality. Love involves the desire to maximize, not minimize, others. In other words, love propels a person to want to elevate and promote people in any way possible. The opposite of wanting to promote and support others (unconditional = love) is to want to silence, push down, and diminish them (hate = racism).

Suggestions for You to Utilize in Resolving Racism in Your Immediate Environment

While I am aware of the arguments for maintaining a segregated society, my experience has taught me that there is one sure solution for resolving the racism in one's immediate environment: contact, contact, contact. There have been countless times in which myself and others have experienced previously prejudiced individuals who have stated how much they learned about their own ignorant beliefs by meeting and talking to someone of color. I am also adamantly against the notion that people of color should buy into the misinformation and negative stereotyping that we have endured for so many years. For example, a pervasive myth about African Americans that we have accepted is the notion that we are horrible in business. I know personally of too many successful black businesswomen and men for this stereotype to be perpetuated by blacks themselves. We shoot ourselves in the foot by helping to keep the lie alive that we are inept and incompetent as a people. These negative statements that we make are perhaps even more damaging than those made about us by others. These ideas are only myths and stereotypes, with little truth in them. Having dealt with many people from many different backgrounds, who have been involved in many kinds of business endeavors, I have been treated well and I have been treated badly by both white-owned and black-owned businesses.

I believe that to alleviate the racism in the immediate environment, we first need to address the ideas that are in our own minds. Do we really believe that a tan makes the difference in the caliber of person? We as a black people need to be aware and not buy into the negatives, so that we will be able to help educate the non-African Americans around us as to the reality of our lives. We also need to remember (every person, those of color and otherwise) that ultimately we affect each other. None of us lives in a vacuum and to hold any person back due to racism, is to hold us all back. After all, it could be the black young woman or man who is not welcomed into the ranks of a prestigious group of all-white scientists, who was meant to discover the cure for AIDS. One never knows, but if racist thought is not continuously addressed and fought with education and exposure, many more people could die unnecessarily, because of those who are too terrified to open their tightly closed minds.

The bottom line is this: In my own mind I conceptualize racism as nothing more than one of many manifestations of low self-regard and an inability to cope with one's own perceived inadequacies. Some of us act out these feelings of self-negativity by doing things to actively hurt ourselves, such as taking harmful drugs or attempting to commit suicide. Others act upon these feelings of self-loathing in passive ways, such as putting others down in order to deflect attention from one's self.

I believe that racism, used as an excuse for perceived inadequacies (whether conscious or not), is true even in terms of economic politics. In this arena many argue that racism serves its purpose in maintaining a poorer class (often but not always people of color) so that the rich (most often, but not always, white) population can step on their backs in order to keep getting richer. It is not a sense of healthy competition in the marketplace that perpetuates these underhanded economic goings on. Rather, the idea that fair competition in the marketplace is replaced by underhanded practices (e.g. racism, discrimination) to keep a certain faction of the population on the outside looking in, is itself a declaration of feeling inferior in what one has to offer. If this were not the case, would not confidence and a belief that the best product/service will win, eliminate the need to undermine the competition using racism . . . or any other means for that matter?

Allow me now to draw this discussion to an end by creating an analogy. Imagine, if you will, a typical, tiny, black ant. This is the kind of ant that a person might see on any sidewalk in the middle of any big city. Now imagine a six-foot, four inch basketball player who was recently drafted by the NBA. Let us assume that this is a young person at the peak of his physical strength and endurance. As this individual walks down a crowded street during the middle of the afternoon, he happens to look down in time to notice the tiny black ant, who is diligently working on an anthill. Now, if the newly drafted NBA player simply walks on, fully confident that he is taller, stronger, and a better athlete than the tiny ant, most of us would probably think nothing of it. On the other hand, if the six foot four inch young person felt an overwhelming need to prove to the world and to himself over and over and over again that he really is better than the ant, we may then become alarmed. The basketball player's overwhelming need to prove that he is stronger than the ant; deemed by God as the one true species and therefore that all ants must be crushed or must serve him because he is after all the greater of the two, might cause others to consider that he may be in need of some form of psychological intervention.

Keep in mind that racist mentality tells us that the "superior" race (represented by the basketball player) is always the more desirable person, and the "inferior" race (represented by the ant) should be feared and kept in its place so as not to cause undue confusion. What is the point of the analogy? If any person is confident in her or his own self-worth, then that confidence eliminates the need to create campaigns of hatred against others. In other words, a healthy self-love allows one to let others be who they are, without feeling threatened by perceived differences. Not long ago, two black psychologists campaigned to have prejudice and racism placed into the psychological diagnostic code as a form of mental illness or psychological depravation. They were unsuccessful in their effort. I believe that they were right on target.

CHAPTER 12
"NO ONE MODEL AMERICAN" STATEMENT: LOOKING AHEAD TO THE FUTURE

Frances V. Rains
Penn State University
University Park, Pennsylvania

M y task is to bring us to future considerations for the *"No One Model American"* statement, issued by the American Association of Colleges of Teacher Education in 1972, and revisited by my coming before you, the daughter of a Japanese War-bride who could not find her Japanese-American relatives who had been interned, because after their release an "invisible" diaspora occurred, and a Choctaw/Cherokee father whose memory of stories shared about the forced removal, relocation, and attempts at genocide have not been forgotten. So, I come not so much to revise the statement, as to reinvasion it in light of issues that not only affect how we teach, but will impact the heart of our nation–our understandings and our actions.

In the brevity of time that I have been given to address this focus, I bring to you only four potential issues–which I see as four interrelated, overlapping circles, much as a Venn diagram in the shape of a four leaf clover. First, I want to briefly touch upon these interrelated circles, and then touch upon how we might re-think our actions.

Four Interrelated Issues that Impact the Future

The four circles represent respectively: Curriculum, Teacher Education Programs, Graduate Education Programs, and Language. "Curriculum" represents some ways curricula is manifested in schools and is connected to the preparation of future teachers through "Teacher Education," and is connected to "Graduate Education Programs" that produce the future professors in Teacher Education. Finally, they are all connected to issues of "Language." These issues represent the tension between "No One Model American" statements and how they are translated and practiced.

There are three prominent situations that many schools find themselves in with regard to student populations and how the *"No One Model American"* statement is, or is not addressed in the "Curriculum" today. Many schools are in the situation of having predominantly white student populations, with little change foreseeable in the next 25 years or so. There is also the situation where many schools have a wide range of visible cultural pluralism in their student populations. Finally, there are many schools that have been historically predominantly white, but for some political or economic reason, have recently experienced an influx of an ethnic group, typically in a large enough number to merit concern by the school/school officials.

In many of the schools that have a predominantly white population, it is possible that the "multicultural" curriculum practices may be what I call "Cultural Voyeurism." There are two major camps within Cultural Voyeurism–the "Tourist/Holidays & Contributions" camp and the "Safety First" camp. In the "Tourist/Holidays & Contributions" camp, it is not uncommon to see the "exotic" or "foods" being the focus of study. So, for example, there might be the eating with chopsticks and having a fortune cookie on Chinese New Year, and the eating of tacos from Taco Bell, while they listen to La Cucaracha on Cinco de Mayo. Another example would be the "I Have a Dream" speech either displayed as a poster, or read aloud for Black History month. On the surface these seem to be an integration of multicultural education, and yet, such curricula is able to ignore the past and present inequities through a sanitized translation of the *"No One Model American"* statement.

At the same time, there are other schools, also with predominantly white student populations, that practice a "Safety First" version of multicultural curricula. An example of this is what I call the "Fab Four." The "Fab Four" are: Harriet Tubman, Sojourner Truth, Rosa Parks, and Martin Luther King. These are the people taught about for Black History month, often in isolation, in ways that valorized them and uphold them as icons. Did these four individuals have a role in our multicultural history? Of course they did. Their effort and hard work made significant contributions to our society. However, by narrowly focusing on the "Fab Four," it is possible to dismiss or ignore the Ida B. Wells, the Frances Harpers, the Emmett Tills, the Megar Fvers, the Fannie Lou Hamers, and the Ella Bakers of the world, along with organizations like SNCC [Student Nonviolent Coordinating Committee] that could empower students in a democratic society, as well as inform them about electric eras of our nation's history.

Another example of the "Safety First" practices, occur in the countless schools where I have supervised field experiences, supervised student teachers, or been invited to give presentations related to Native Americans. Typically, in the month of November, I am very popular as a Native woman, and am asked to give presentations in elementary classrooms, often next to "tee pees" at Thanksgiving, never mind that the Wampanoags did not live in tee pees. In many such schools, Native peoples are taught as if Columbus had not arrived yet. In such settings, Natives are studied as regional groupings that are compared and contrasted on transportation, clothing, food, and entertainment differences and similarities, as if the white Man had not set foot on the continent. These practices ignore the conquest, greed, and attempts at genocide that are also a part of our collective American history.

A second situation occurs in schools where the student population is visibly very pluralistic. Yet, look closely at how pluralistic the "gifted and talented," or the "college-bound" courses are. These "tracks" typically do not mirror the pluralism of the student body.

Ironically, I was told that I should consider the vocational education track in seventh grade. I didn't listen (and have since earned a Ph.D.), but I was not advised about such critical fundamentals of the college track, such as taking the ACT or SAT for college entrance, until after the deadlines for such criteria had passed. And my experience is not unique among many youth of color. The prominence of the hidden curriculum and tracking in such school situations often ignores the curricular content, as well as the *"No One Model American"* statement.

The third situation that affects many schools is the circumstance where their student population has historically been predominantly white, but for some political or economic reason, there is an influx of an ethnic group, typically in too large of a number to ignore. Typically this influx occurs at the lower end of the socio-economic level, often lower than the remaining school population. Here such schools often apply a "radical Band-Aid," focused on scrambling to find the instructional strategies to cope with the different needs of the students. What often gets lost in the mix is the curricula content and how the *"No One Model American"* statement relates to the school and the students.

Besides curriculum, there is the interrelated issue of teacher education. There are three situations at the Teacher Education level that merit reflection. There is the "single course" model, the "integration" model, and the enrollment issue. All three relate to how the statement of *"No One Model American"* is or is not addressed at this level. In the "single course" model, a "cultural diversity" type course may be required by the Teacher Education program, however, it is also possible that this course is unconnected to the actual preparation of future teachers. For example, there are colleges of Teacher Education that require that a "cultural diversity" course be taken as a prerequisite of the program. However, in my experience, this course is often taken in the freshman or sophomore year in the broad area of general education. The difficulty with this model is that the cultural diversity course is not connected to the Teacher Education program, and little effort may be made to make that connection in or through the program design. It is often seen by advisees as just one more thing to check off of their list. In such circumstances, I have had student advisees ask, "Which one is the easiest to take?" This translation does little to enhance or capture the essence of the *"No One Model American"* statement.

On the other hand, there is the "integration" model adopted by some Teacher Education programs. This, unfortunately, too often gets played out as the "if I have time on December 18, I will give it a half hour of coverage, but if I run out of time, that will be the first thing to go" practice. Although integration (called "infusion" in the *"No One Model American"* statement) was a key component of these statements, the translation and practice seems a far cry from the original intent.

In Teacher Education there is also the issue of enrollment. If the current trend is any indication of the near future, the enrollments in Teacher Education are likely to continue to be predominantly white, mono-cultural, upper middle class females. What is being done to ensure that the *"No One Model American"* statement intent and focus is delivered to these mostly white females in a meaningful way? And equally important, what is being done to honor the statement regarding the vital importance of having a diverse student population? That is, what is being done *by* Teacher Education programs to ensure that future enrollments are not homogeneously white, female, middle class and mono-cultural, as a pluralistic student population has been an essential component of the statement?

"Graduate Education Programs," that prepare the next generation of future professors in education, are not immune from scrutiny in how the statement gets translated and practiced. In Graduate programs there are three areas worthy of review. "Faculty resistance," "no requirement," and "student resistance" all merit consideration in light of the future of the "No One Model American" statement.

Faculty resistance, as the term implies, is resistance by faculty to the concepts behind the statement. Some might interpret it as a threat to their academic freedom and reject the need to address the statement or its intent within their courses. Others may see it as turf battles of time, and whose turf it is considered to be. An example from a faculty meeting in one graduate program area that I attended might shed some light on this subject. In this meeting I raised the question, as a new faculty member, of the graduate program's commitment to "diversity." Wherein, a colleague proceeded to get immediately irate and demand to know what type of "diversity" I was talking about. He went on to state, in an angry tone, that there was "economic diversity," and "gender diversity" and so on. The Chair of the department cut in and suggested that I be made the chair of a committee that would be in charge of collecting all of the syllabi generated by the faculty in this particular department in order to determine who mentioned "diversity" in their syllabus. He added that it would help the department with the university's strategic plan on diversity. I raise this issue because I am a junior professor, and to bring the matter up among senior colleagues when I am on tenure track is risky. Yet, the development of future professors in education should be the responsibility of all, according to the statement. And given that the statement has been in effect since 1972, it would not seem that novel to raise the concept of faculty commitment to diversity, nor should I be reduced to being the "diversity police" for syllabi so long after the "No One Model American" statement had been established.

Sadly, many graduate programs of education do not have a culture diversity requirement of any kind. This means that unless a graduate student seeks out such a course in another program area on his or her own, often as an elective, then it is quite possible for a graduate student to become a professor in Education without any prior coursework in cultural pluralism. In some cases, graduate students may even be advised against taking such a course, as there is not a perceived need, nor benefit, to the program area, according to some graduate advisors.

In some graduate programs that do require a course, there is what I call "student resistance," which materializes as an exemptions tactic used by students who resist the necessity of the requirement. You may have seen this played out where you are. A graduate student states that he or she has been to Europe, and maybe even names a specific country [read: as a tourist]. The graduate student may even go so far as to state that he or she visited a beer garden in Germany, or spent two whole weeks in Spain, and therefore should be exempt from the requirement. Another strategy that has been utilized by some graduate students is the "but I speak _____ " exemption tactic. This is where a graduate student speaks a "foreign" language [this does not take into consideration the quality of the language acquisition and level of language communication skills], typically a romance language, and expects that the language somehow immunizes him or her from having to take such a course. Both the tourism and the foreign language approaches, when compounded by faculty resistance, indicate that the statement has not been translated into effective means of implementation at the graduate level.

Finally, there is the overlapping issue of "Language." Here I will address only three terms related to the *"No One Model American"* statements. The terms are: "multicultural" education [read: very safe]; "global" [read: "we study Japan, so what's the problem?"]; and "diversity" [read: "Gee, but everyone's unique"– freckles, baldness, weight, height, etc. all become unique identifiers that 'represent' "diversity"]. In effect, these terms have become neutralized on the one hand, and overloaded with their own baggage on the other. In either case, the status quo remains unexamined, and the inequalities that have existed can continue unabated. The focus and intent of the statement are thereby undermined.

In light of these issues that we carry forth into the new millennium, we must re-envision how we proceed. I say "proceed" because I believe in *ACTIONS* and I am concerned that the statements in the past has lacked "teeth"–not to diminish the hard work that went into the original statement, nor how radical it was at the time–but rather to think about where we are now. So, consider this a CALL TO ACTION related to the following: We need a *RE-THINKING of what constitutes history*, from a history that is from a predominantly white and male approach that goes from war to war, to a history that reflects the interactions, conflicts, contributions *between and among* groups, *and* that accurately reflects not only the "good," but also how power, privilege, and oppression have operated to advantage and benefit some, at the cost of oppressing or attempting to annihilate others. It *IS* the history of America! We must throw back the curtains on the narrow images of history to show and teach our chil-

dren HONESTLY–THE *FULL* HISTORY OF AMERICA–that helps them to understand how race, class and gender intersect–past and present.

We need a RE-THINKING of how we teach about social, cultural, and economic inequities, past and present, in ways that challenge the "status quo," "busi-
ness-as-usual" approach. This approach has permitted the contributions, heroes, and
holidays to be taught in isolation, rather than embedded in a context of power and
oppression. Also thoughts of WHO BENEFITS, HOW, and WHY, and of WHO
LOSES, HOW, and WHY ARE-THINKING of TEACHER EDUCATION and
GRADUATE PROGRAMS is necessary to ensure future teachers and future education professors have adequate background knowledge necessary to teach and reach in
the new millennium. At the same time, these future teachers and professors need
assistance to learn and understand how to utilize that knowledge in ways that impact
curricula, instructional practices, hidden curriculum, and tracking, while at the same
time introduces them to the "best practices" and useful research.

Finally, a RE-THINKING of terminology is also needed as we move into the
new millennium, with attention to the fluidness and shifts that occur within language. More importantly, we need to be attentive to the power dynamics of language, *not* to focus on the *"politically correct,"* but rather to understand better *the
meanings and substance behind the words* and the *baggage* they may carry.

As with many of the Japanese American families that had been interned, my
mother's relatives–due to many complicated reasons–had been separated during the
internment period. After the internment they had to first find each other, and then as
they were able to re-group, most of the family decided to relocate in the Chicago
area, with one son who had been in the 442nd going back to live in Seattle–where the
family had lived before the internment began. After some searching, and frustration,
my mother was able to eventually find her "American" relatives there in Chicago.

There are many interrelated issues that are vital to consider in reflecting upon
the "No One Model American" statement. It is not the intent here to list them all,
rather to touch *upon* those that in the interest of time, have potential relevance for
those who work with some aspect of Multicultural Education.

I am indebted to Dr. Christine Sleeter for our conversation, at this conference,
regarding this matter. I have asked her permission to include this in my chapter.

CHAPTER 13
FAMILY RACISM

Marie Love
The Union Institute
Cincinnati, Ohio

When I was asked to write about racism from my personal experiences, I initially drew a blank. I am a white American. How could I encounter racism? I drew from the stereotype that racism is something only black Americans experience. Today, being a family therapist, the subject of racism should have immediately risen to my consciousness. It is easy to suppress experiences that cause personal pain. But as you learn and after careful examination, I realized that I was exposed to racism in my family at an early age.

Although the black experience of racism is different from the white experience, I hope to draw some parallel experiences so we may all learn from each other. I hope to help others to understand that within the black culture, as well as within other ethnic cultures, a varied racist experience can occur. Awareness is an enormous factor in overcoming and understanding our past experiences.

I would like to discuss racism in a cultural context. Culture influences our behavior toward others and our personal beliefs. Cultural exposure in our early years has an enormous impact, often in an implicit or unconscious way. Our self-concept is formed in the early years. The self-concept is composed of all the beliefs and attitudes that have been imposed upon us. Our early cultural experiences can impact our thinking processes as to who we are and what we are capable of becoming. These formulated opinions, if negative and left unchallenged, can become our internalized self-concept. The cultural exposure must be analyzed in a larger framework. The cultural context includes one's race, gender, nationality, and ethnicity. Actually, the term "culture" is far-reaching to include economics, religion, family structure, rituals, music, food, clothing, religion, values, education, code of conduct, sexual preference, and occupation (the list goes on and on). Within a broad cultural context, individuals can and do experience racism. After all, all cultures have a certain "we are better than they are" element. Within the same cultural context, the racism experience may be different. Throughout our journey in life, when we encounter differences, we may experience a form of cultural racism. Only by our developing an awareness of its existence, an understanding of ourselves and others, acknowledgement of individual differences, and developing skills to overcome stereotyping will we achieve a culture free from racism.

My personal story will discuss racism from my ethnicity. My mother is of Italian-American descent. My father emigrated from Southern Italy at the age of 21. The acknowledgement of the terms "Italian descent" and "immigrated" can be used as racial barriers. Racism is used as a dividing factor for individuals. It sets up a win-lose situation. It creates the attitude that if one is good, then the other must be bad. It is a form of power and control over other individuals. The experience is of the dehumanization of individuals. Instead of looking for commonalties, we seek to find differences. As an emigrant, my father was different. He had to learn the English language. He spoke with a noticeably Italian accent. I was never sure of his command of written English. The natural barriers created by his emigration enabled other, naturally born American family members to further exploit their racist views. An interesting irony to the story relates to my friends' reactions toward my father. My friends were from varied backgrounds, with American-born parents. They loved coming into our home. My father greeted my friends with hugs and open expressions of warmth. His expression of hugs and kisses was natural in his culture. My friends' fathers did not openly express affection. As a pre-adolescent, my friends were an important part of my life. From my friends' acceptance of my father, I learned to understand that being different was okay.

As my father entered the business world, I am sure his differences created experiences of racism. To combat this experience, he studied for many years at night school to develop a command of the language, as well as a trade. His unique differences of speaking in a non-native language were ever-present. My father never openly expressed anger at his personal experiences. He was forever grateful to be an American citizen, and celebrated every Fourth of July by displaying an American flag.

I began thinking about my personal encounter with racism. When did I remember and what did I remember? We do have to be invited into our thinking processes to rediscover the painful encounters, and sometimes-subtle experiences, of our cultural racism. My encounters of racism happened within our extended family. My mother's three sisters married Americans born from German, Spanish, and Italian heritage. The fourth sister married a native-born Italian who immigrated from Northern Italy. Our family was different. The racist experience within my family made the encounters even more painful. I was raised to respect my family and adults.

At about age 10, I remember stories of my cousins' families. The prevailing themes all focused upon the high educational levels within the families and grandparents. I never met my grandparents from my father's family. They lived in Italy. I was made aware of my grandparents through photographs. The family themes of being college-educated and being light-skinned were considered a high value. Regional ethnic culture creates different views within families. Being from Southern Italy was not valued within my extended family yet; my father immigrated from Southern Italy. The praise and glory of Northern Italy was spoken within our family. My one uncle was from the North. This is an example of regional racism within the same country. The comparisons between the North and the South continued in our family. I loved and respected my father. It was confusing for me as a child to hear negative comments concerning our ethnicity. I did not understand the words. Why were they saying these things? Why was this happening within our family? Why weren't we valued in our family?

My grandfather and aunt on my mother's side had blond hair coloring. The hair color of my aunt and grandfather was valued in our family. Being a dark haired medium-skin toned girl in this family was difficult. It took many years for me to sort out what should be valued in individuals. The messages I received at home were different from those of the extended family. As I developed an awareness of the toxic culture I was subjected to, I was able to understand and develop knowledge of the meaningless values imposed upon me as a young child. Later in life I developed the skills to communicate my thoughts combating our family's raciest views. These years were the most enjoyable for me.

Reflecting upon my previous dialogue, it seems so ridiculous that such statements held power. It is a lesson in understanding the importance of spoken words to children, and the power that words convey. I think my understanding in working with children was formulated by my early experiences of cultural racism. I will remember the impact of these words spoken to children. My studying family therapy was a direct consequence of surviving my experiences. I wanted to develop an understanding of the family's power and influence upon individuals. It is amazing that many voices spoken in unison can be so misleading. I now understand that this is a direct result of a learned culture within a family. As I work with families I try to search for different voices within the family so they may be heard and honored. I think direct experience can be a powerful tool in learning. I developed a keen awareness that labeling individuals is harmful. I carried this experience into my personal life. When I had children, a boy and a girl, I was aware of gender being used to divide individuals. I learned to question teacher's expectations concerning capabilities of boys and girls. I learned that teachers are part of a cultural environment. I learned to question teacher's voices even though they spoke in unison.

Cultural racism can be experienced outside the extended family. My one uncle had such an experience. He spoke English well. He was an engineer with a graduate degree educated in Italy. He met my aunt as her American father was employed temporarily in Italy. Upon entering the United States, he had a difficult time finding a job. While being interviewed by a large American company, he was given papers to be processed in the employment office. He carefully lifted the top paper and read the following, "Do not hire this man. He is a foreigner!" I still remember the expression on his face as he recounted the story. My uncle was never able to secure a job matching his qualifications.

In analyzing final statements on racism, several learned experiences come into the picture. One pertaining to the success of my father in a business community made me keenly aware of many factors. An individual can be successful through motivation, an openness to learn and a desire to be challenged. An attitude of openness as to what the world offers and disagreeing with other people's perceptions enables us to overcome barriers of racism. We prosper by not allowing toxic words to define us. We place our expectations and priorities as achievable goals. We develop a strong self-concept based on our achievements, and not others' negative definitions of us.

What else did I learn from my personal experiences? I learned that racist individuals will always find subjects. By subjects, I mean individuals "to treat as less than themselves." Racist individuals will look for divisive measures to separate individuals. They are not looking for solutions, but a creation of "teams" consisting of other individuals to support their ideas. The concept of "power in numbers" seems applicable to racist individuals.

It seems that another concept in racist individuals seems to be the concept of change. They find change difficult. Change implies a shift perhaps in the power of an individual or group. A chance to break a stereotype can be an outcome of the change process. Change can bring on a newly formed awareness. Change can imply people coming together for a common good. It is a power shift. With change come new skills to learn to accommodate a new process. With these experiences, the idea of protecting young children from racist views becomes paramount. We understand the developing phase of their self-concept and the vulnerability of young children to the spoken word. We can train young children to look at the word "differences" as a natural happening.

We celebrate different seasons. Different flowers and smells refresh us. The interest of different faces is an amazing wonder. The lists of different celebrations are endless. It is important to understand that children are capable of understanding differing opinions. Although it is complicated at first, children have the capacity to later sort out information and form their opinions. What is important is that children have a strong support in the home. Unfortunately, today, many children do not have this support system. They come from poverty, with mothers trying to survive. Why are our children living in poverty in this vast country? Do we feel that children are capable of supporting themselves? Why are our children the poorest group in this country? These questions pose an obstacle for solving racism in this country.

CHAPTER 14
A WINNER NEVER QUITS AND A
QUITTER NEVER WINS
'CUZ MY DADDY SAID SO

Celina Echols
Southeastern Louisiana University
Hammond, Louisiana

The following treatise is one of many essays by black professional women across America. *The Anthology of Black Women's Voices* contains the writers' first, and many subsequent encounters with racism, and how they have learned to survive. This essay also includes vernacular akin to the culture of Louisiana but specifically the African American culture. The author retains the right to use the words *black* and *African American* interchangeably to portray her appreciation of cultural identity philosophy advocated during the civil rights era and a more contemporary approach that relates people to their specific continent or country of origin.

Sociocultural and historical influences affect human development in both negative and positive ways. These influences may include the following: the role of the elderly in the family, the presence or absence of father and mother, parenting styles, income, level of peer interaction, and urban verses rural place of residency. The development of African Americans living in the United States can be most heavily influenced by racism. This reflective essay gives accounts of my experience with racism and how I have learned to survive as an African American woman living in the United States. My first racial experience is as vivid in my memory as if it had happened yesterday. However, let me first provide a sociocultural and historical framework, and then share a little about my upbringing in order to put the racial experiences into perspective.

I am a native of the South, the second of four children (a son and three daughters) of parent educators. My father and mother are both oldest siblings from large families, graduates of historically *black* institutions, and both assisted in the rearing of their younger siblings. Both of my parents' parents sharecropped from whites for many years. My father's parents lost 200 acres of land in the early 1900s due to the local tax assessor's wrongful assessment of their land, based upon what he assumed to be the value of the family's material possessions. My grandparents were the first blacks in the county to own a Model T, an organ, and many possessions considered luxury items. It was these items and others that caused an additional assessment of taxes, and the subsequent loss of land.

Shortly after my parents' marriage, they moved to an area 30 miles from the location of Mack Parker's lynching. One Saturday afternoon when my father was in Baton Rouge attending graduate school, my mother was talking to her sister-in-law by phone when a white man drove into the driveway. My mother, with one hand on a pistol and the other on a handle of a butcher's knife, told her sister-in-law a "white devil" had driven up. She asked my aunt's permission to end their conversation so that she could inquire about his presence. The man asked if he could borrow some gas because his car had "run out of gas." My mother was in her last trimester of pregnancy. She passed an empty milk jug through a half closed door and gestured for him to take some gas from the parked car but leave the jug on the porch when he had finished. However, when he finished, he came back and asked her how much money could he "give for some of that." He pointed towards her vaginal area. She responded, "I'm telling my husband. You'd better leave" and slammed the door. That night, my parent's home was sprayed with gun fire. During this same time, my father was striving to obtain a Master of Education degree. There were no state institutions granting African Americans graduate degrees, therefore, my father was forced to commute every weekend to Southern University in Baton Rouge, Louisiana. He describes these times as "hot in Mississippi." He recounts, as a civil rights worker, activists were often told if a car drove behind you with the head beams on high (possibly Klan men looking for a black to lynch) one should drive like a "bat out of hell." Father says there was not a night that he didn't leave Baton Rouge without an intense feeling in the pit of his stomach. One of the towns he had to drive through was Magnolia, Mississippi. Magnolia once had a sign posted with these words, "Don't let the sun set in Magnolia if your skin is black."

In the summer of 1969, my parents bought 60 acres of land previously owned by a white man who told my father he sold it to him to infuriate his family who didn't want him to sale to "coloreds." In the summer of 1969, my mother also gave birth to my youngest sister. There is a tendency in African American families for children within the same family to have varying skin complexions. This is the result of the sexual interactions between slaves and their masters during the colonial period. My sister was born with light brown skin and fine, curly hair. My other siblings and I were much darker with nappier hair. I thought my sister was much prettier than me. Therefore, I would stand at her crib and pinch her to make her cry. Her crying made me feel better because of our color differences. I didn't understand the differences, but I knew my sister looked different than the rest of us. In the summer of 1969, my father's two younger sisters visited Mississippi from California. I was five years of age, and in total awe of my aunts who drank liquor and smoked (but not in front of Daddy). They smelled of expensive colognes and they didn't speak with southern accents. My aunts were sophisticated, and they washed and pressed my hair, then trimmed the split ends for a bang (Mamma never did this).

One afternoon my aunts asked Daddy to borrow his 1953 yellow Chevrolet pick-up to take the nieces and nephews to town for ice cream. The county seat was approximately 13 miles from where we had recently moved. The children were excited at the prospect of going to town for ice cream. Buying fast-food was something our parents never did. My parents felt it was more economical to buy large quantities of food rather than going to town for such a luxury at a higher price. The children climbed into the back of the pick-up and my aunts drove to town. We parked in front of the deli and my aunts sent my oldest male cousin to get the ice cream so that we could eat in the truck as we drove back home. I cannot remember how long he was away from the truck but it was for some time because my aunts became concerned about his welfare. Just as they were about to leave the truck to check on him, he came away from the deli, ice cream in hand, and a look of confusion and mounting anger. My aunts asked what happened and he said, "They wouldn't give me the ice cream because they asked if ice cream is what I came for." I said, "Yes." They said, "Well, you are not going to get it until you say yes Ma'am to us." My cousin refused to say it and subsequently didn't get the ice cream. When he gave in, he got the ice cream. My aunts were furious. We had begun to eat our ice cream between their angry exclamation of "things have not changed one bit down here. Rednecks will always be rednecks." One aunt even said she wished she had known what my cousin was experiencing before he paid for the ice cream. I was glad they didn't know. We might not have gotten the ice cream. We had not even traveled two miles when we were pulled over by a state trooper who gave my aunts a ticket for speeding five miles over the speed limit. My aunts swore us children to secrecy about the ticket. But, immediately after arriving at my grandmother's home, I climbed unto my father's lap and told him about the incident. My father hugged me tightly and assured me things were going to be all right.

By fall 1969, I was anxious to begin school. My mother would be my first grade teacher. Both my parents taught at an all black school despite the Supreme Court decision that the policy of *separate but equal* was unconstitutional. Mississippi was one of the few states that believed itself to be sovereign, without accountability to the federal government or the U.S. Supreme Court. Therefore, despite the Court's decision, Mississippi public school districts continued to practice a policy of separate but equal. However, when I returned to school after Christmas break, Mississippi was mandated to integrate its schools. For the first time in my life I was attending schools with whites. The unique difference in this mandatory integration is that white teachers taught white students, and black teachers taught black children. Every day the halls were sprayed with insecticide. "We" assumed the spraying was to rid the halls and rooms of insects brought by blacks; for after that year, the daily spraying ceased. The federal government insisted that separate classrooms by race must change to racially inclusive classes. My mother was angry at this and other treatment she experienced at the administrative level (example: administrative request to list all community and civic organization in which you held membership, including the NAACP). In an act of silent defiance and pride, she sewed wonderful African dashikis and wore them to school.

White people in the South have always liked for blacks (in particular) to show respect by saying, "yes, Ma'am." However, my parents told their children we could say, "yes" and "no" as long as we said it politely. We did not have to apply sir and ma'am. Children were often spanked if they didn't adhere to the Ma'am and Sir. However, my siblings were never spanked. Perhaps because most local educators knew my parents. In 1971, I entered my first class of racially mixed students. I vividly remember the black girls and boys wanting to touch white students' hair. My black classmates would wear sweaters on their hair to imitate white girls having hair long enough to swing from one side to the other. I also remember an argument that ensued between a white female students and myself about my hair "looking like a sheep's wool" and my outcry that "at least mine doesn't look like a pony's tail." By sixth grade, my Mississippi History teacher insisted that I say, "yes, Sir" to him, and I politely explained to him what my parents had said. He called a woman teacher in to administer corporal punishment. As she picked up the paddle, he stopped her hand in mid-stream and said, "Lillie, let her go." He abruptly sent me back to class and made me sit in the corner during class. I was not permitted to interact with other children for the remainder of the day. Once home, I told my parents what happened. To this day, I have no idea what transpired, but my father visited school and met the teacher and principal. The next day I was allowed to sit and interact with other students. However, I remember until high school graduation day, being hatefully stared at by the teacher.

At home, several incidents took place between 1971 and 1981. We came home from school one afternoon to find our yard aflame. Someone spray painted "KKK" on the asphalt road in front of our home. On several occasions someone would drive into the front yard, remain for several minutes, and drive away. White males began drag racing their cars in front of our house. One of our dogs was poisoned. Despite my father being known by many in our county of residence, and respected for his lack of tolerance for alcohol consumption, he was humiliated by police one afternoon. He was stopped, searched, made to take a breathalyzer test, and a walking sobriety test on the main street of our town. He was allegedly "weaving while driving." One Sunday afternoon, an elderly white neighbor came by to see my father. My brother went to the driveway to inquire of his needs. The man exclaimed, "boy is your pappy home?" My brother said, "I don't have a pappy." My brother was determined not to acknowledge the belittling of my father's position and the neighbor would not change his approach. Needless to say, when my brother returned to family dinner and explained what happened, he was so filled with anger he could not eat. The neighbor did not visit my father that day.

To many of our neighbors, I guess my family was somewhat of a novelty. Our social interaction was well guarded by my parents. Education was highly valued. My parents believed in attending social, church, and school events with their children. As children, our interaction lay primarily with cousins and people who my parents felt wanted their "children to do something constructive in life."

By the time I entered my senior year of high school, there were no students I considered friends except two white males who were quite academically focused. One student I would learn later shares my bloodline. The other student was a native of a mid-western state. Our interaction was positive and yet often argumentative. Frequently we engaged in conversation relative to the civil war, Vietnam, and civil rights. I approached these two students and other members of the senior class about having a prom. Students had never had an integrated prom at the county's public schools. Black seniors had their "get-together" and white students had their "get-together." We wrote letters to the local school board. We arranged meetings with the principals. We talked to the student government association. Finally, the Board of Education left the decision to the principals. The predominately black school's principal agreed. The principal of the school that I attended said, "no." I asked for a private meeting with him where I reminded him of the day when he welcomed us as high school seniors. He said we were now old enough to ask for explanations when told we should or should not do certain things. I asked him if the reason he didn't want us to have a prom is because he didn't want blacks and whites dancing together. He turned red, pushed me out of his office, and exclaimed, "You are instigating racial problems." Needless-to-say, there was no senior prom but the following class was finally able to have a racially integrated senior prom.

I think my experience at a predominately white state institution is typical for many blacks attending white universities. I was proud to attend an institution where a black man fought to gain access to higher education, yet suffered fatally at the hands of racists who wanted to prohibit his pursuit of higher education. I took pride in advocating the integration of the Pan Hellenic dorm by the AKA sorority. I took pride in advocating against the flying of the confederate flag during football games. I questioned my career ambitions when working with the campus television station and was told that I sounded "too black." The finale of all these incidents was when one of the university's highly prized black football players was accused of raping a white female student. Forensic evidence was eventually able to assist the defense in proving its case and acquitting the student, but not before the career of a potentially great athlete was destroyed.

Two and a half years ago, I was invited to join the faculty at a predominately white institution. I was not enthusiastic with the interview but was encouraged by my major professors to consider the invitation. I did as they suggested. My first semester students started a letter writing campaign alleging many of the following things about me: racist, using words one cannot find in the dictionary, talks about diversity and multiculturalism too much, suggests that we argue in class, and too much home work at the undergraduate level.

By now, if you are not a person of color, I hope you have some understanding about what it meant when James Baldwin said, "being black in America is an objective reality." When most Americans see a person of African descent, the first thing they see is the color of the individual's skin with little knowledge about what constitutes who is the person. The negative (though covert pressure) of racism makes being black in America something that has to be contended with daily. The incidents I have mentioned are only a few of those experienced if one considers 365 days multiplied by my age. How do I enjoy life when I realize racism is so interwoven in my daily interactions with others? I recommend several things: belief in God, belief in self, support of family and friends, and the commitment to educate.

Change is intricate and methodical in comparison with the average life-span of humans. However, belief in God enables one to understand that negativity from today and yesterday can change the future when good overcomes evil, I focus on the positives of life, and I respond proactively to create my own limitless future.

When there are university functions to which "we" are invited but hesitate to attend, because "we" are the only ones of color, we limit our knowledge about resources that may be available to us, and eliminate opportunities to add value to the lives of others because of our diversity. We must be mindful that before we attend such gatherings, we need to know the expected purpose of the program. Then, we must make a decision to positively impact our surrounding with our words, actions, and attitudes.

Very few things happen in the human experience without God showing us evidence of the occurrence before it happens. The problem is that humans often do not acknowledge the attitudes, behaviors, and actions within their social sphere. Standing still, listening, and taking appropriate action is not a part of our problem solving strategies. When I returned to the South from attending graduate school in the Midwest, I knew, based upon many past racial incidents, what I might expect. I knew many students were not accustomed to interacting with a black professional woman who was quite confident with her subject area and heritage. The messenger and the message were discomforting for many students and they reacted to both. It was up to me to respond to their reaction. I could leave, keep silent, or make a plan "B" for the plan "A" that didn't work. I choose to make a plan "B" for the plan "A." The message is the same but the melody is different. Consequently, student and faculty acceptance is becoming more apparent.

It is equally important to profess our desire for good, and subsequently to work to make good things happen. Working to make things happen involves surrounding ourselves with people who have values akin to ours and challenges us to grow. Sometimes I find the need to "be" with only black folks. I can "be" the way I want to "be" at a just-us-demanded "pawtee." However, one must be mindful of who might attend these functions as well. It is important to surround myself with those who I can relate to culturally, and who often challenge me to continue on my journey of educating underrepresented children.

Collective efforts, thoughts, and purposes are empowering. I believe my fore-parents' belief that God would intervene in their plights of chattel slavery, black codes, apartheid, segregation, and other mechanisms of disfranchisement has availed me. My foreparents may not have been the immediate beneficiaries of His blessings, but as their offspring, I can carry a belief of hope to my children. Herein lies the belief that is my father's testament to life: *A Winner Never Quits and a Quitter Never Wins*. When I speak to colleagues about whether racism in America has changed, I often find they are disgruntled with the "small effects" that remain from efforts gained during the civil rights movement. My contention is that African Americans cannot lose hope. We must trust God and ask for His guidance, take personal responsibility for the present and the future, know the world's history, and rise above every negative situation in life by impacting those around us in a productive fashion, because a "winner never quits and a quitter never wins."

CHAPTER 15
A NATIONAL PERSPECTIVE:
STANDARDIZED TESTING FOR
FOSTERING CULTURAL DIVERSITY
OF EDUCATIONAL OPPORTUNITY
ENLIGHTENMENT

Neil T. Faulk
McNeese State University
Lake Charles, Louisiana

As a child I can remember biking across town to visit a boyhood friend. It was not long after I arrived that my friend and I were engaged in a friendly, but competitive game of one-on-one basketball. Being quite skilled at basketball and much quicker and more agile than my friend, I thought I would easily prevail and win this friendly game. To my dismay I realized that I was actually at a disadvantage rather than an advantage. You see, my friend had grown accustomed to practicing and shooting at his very own basketball goal in his very own backyard. He knew all the intricate little secrets of how to dribble on his cement court and how to shoot the ball with less force against a goal that had the supports cemented into the ground. I was unfamiliar with the type of court and the type of goal that my friend had grown accustomed to. He had the home court advantage.

This was a very strange scenario to me since my backyard basketball court was of dirt and my goal had a lot of "give" in it because it had not been cemented into the ground. My dad had put my goal together with his own two hands, but my friend's goal had been purchased at a sporting goods store. The setting was just not the same. In addition to the setting being quite different, it was also apparent that my friend had his own homemade rules that applied to his specific court. (Kids will do this when playing games–make their own rules to give themselves an advantage.)

I had fun that day, playing at my friend's court. It was a bit frustrating because I knew I was a much better basketball player, yet I struggled, and even lost a game or two that day. Later that afternoon my dad asked me how I had done. Well I told him, especially the parts about the cement court, the different goal, and the homemade rules that my friend had used on his court to his advantage. My dad laughed and told me that is how life is sometimes, and that I would have to adjust to different courts, different settings, and to different people who were much different from myself. Little did I realize how correct he was.

Many years later I was faced with a similar scenario. I had applied to graduate school at several universities to hopefully pursue a Doctorate degree. I was required to take the GRE. Being from a small Cajun community in extreme South Louisiana, I found my experience taking the GRE to be rather frustrating. I found it hard to believe that this test was a true indicator of my graduate school success–since I had earned a 4.0 on Masters degree and also a 4.0 on my Education Specialist degree. I even took the GRE a second time hoping to score much higher–yet not scoring much higher the second or third time. This was indeed a very frustrating experience.

I was eventually accepted into a fine doctoral graduate school, and after one full year of 4.0 academic performance I decided to take the GRE one more time. I once again did not improve my score much at all. I actually scored below the national average yet I eventually earned a Doctorate degree with a 4.0 average. I was so pleased to graduate yet so puzzled at how I could have scored so low on the GRE, yet done so well at a major university with such a fine academic reputation. I thank God that I did not believe the results of the GRE because it indicated that I was a failure waiting to happen–yet I succeeded.

Today, I sit here and wonder how many students from different cultural and ethnic backgrounds are turned away from higher education due to low ACT, SAT, or GRE scores. How many of these students never attend college, or never attempt getting a graduate degree because of low standardized test scores. You see, my cultural background is not the same as the ivory-towered, middle-aged, male Caucasian Ph.D.'s in the northeastern United States who construct these tests. My grandmother did not speak English and did not wish to speak English. She was of mixed Cajun and Indian-American descent, as were many along the bayous of Louisiana in the past. Both of my parents are bilingual, speaking broken English and Cajun French. My cultural experiences were much different than those who construct the standardized tests. Taking the GRE was similar to playing basketball on a foreign court and playing by someone else's rules. The ivory-towered, middle-aged, male Caucasian Ph.D.'s in the Northeast are allowed to put their culture and ethnicity above the ethnicity of all other Americans. All other ethnic groups are forced to play by their rules or fail, even though the other ethnic groups have not been acculturated to the so called "mainstream" test culture of the test makers.

It is no wonder that minority groups do not do well on these so called predictor tests. The tests themselves favor a certain culture, and disfavor other cultures and ethnicities. Perhaps a solution to this dilemma would be to devise an inverse scale since there appears to be an inverse relationship between those who are not in the mainstream culture and the test scores. The inverse scale of measurement would require higher scores of those in the mainstream culture and lower scores of those who are not in the mainstream culture. This would take away some of the home court advantage of the mainstreamers and it would level the playing field of the non-mainstreamers who are at a disadvantage because they are playing on a foreign court and by foreign rules. The further a person's ethnicity from the mainstream, the lower that person's score could be since he/she is playing (testing) in a totally different setting.

While there are those who would be totally against this, I am sure there would be many who would agree. Probably the best solution to this whole problem would be to stop giving standardized test scores so much weight in the evaluation process. If we continue to give so much weight to standardized test scores it would appear that there should be different scales.

I sometimes wonder why minority groups do not protest more loudly when standardized tests are administered. The tests apparently give preference to certain cultures, to the detriment of other cultural ethnic groups. This would make the tests both racially and culturally biased. Yet the testing continues and so many bright minds are being turned away due to the misinformation of standardized test results. I can only imagine testing Jesus Christ on his morality using a paper and pencil standardized test devised by a few ivory-towered, middle aged, male Caucasian Ph.D.s in the Northeast–sort of an invalid test don't you think?

In conclusion, I would hope that all educators and administrators making educated decisions interpret test results with some limits. It is totally unfair to test all groups of people on the same test, especially if the test is devised by people from the mainstream culture. Special training should be applied to those who interpret test results–so that bias and misinformation of test results is stopped. It is a terrible thing to turn away a bright mind and deny an opportunity to someone because of his/her unique ethnicity. We in American education should appreciate the ethnic diversity of our students rather than punish those who are different by denying them the opportunity to advance through the use of standardized testing.

Finally, you may choose to disagree with me. That is your right. However, I wonder how it could be that I scored below the national average on the GRE, yet attended a large major university and scored highest in many of the classes, while those who scored extremely higher on the GRE struggled to make a satisfactory passing grade in many classes. What could have been invalid? You make your own decision. It was also extremely frustrating to be denied fellowships and other academic monetary assistance because of my low GRE scores. Yet, I knew several graduate students who were awarded thousands of dollars worth of scholarships and fellowships because of their high GRE scores. These same (high GRE) students would score less on the classroom tests taken to pass courses to earn a Doctorate. I even tutored some of these (high GRE) students in Statistics and Research-oriented courses. This situation was ridiculous. Here I was working two jobs trying to finance my way through graduate school and at the same time tutoring students who had fifteen-thousand dollar fellowships because of their high GRE scores. Yet my low GRE scores barely got me accepted into graduate school. I felt as if I was being punished for being from a unique cultural and ethnic heritage. I can only imagine how racial minority groups must feel under our system of standardized cultural inequality in testing. Of course, this could only happen in our American educational system where we give all an equal, or not so equal, opportunity. I would hope that in the future that the rules, the courts, and the requirements are the same for all, regardless of cultural or ethnic background.

DATE DUE

OCT 30 2005			